TO Alex,

The cmdr-IN-chieF

Always be blessed!

Rld Ott

Whatever happened to the Promised Land?

Whatever happened to the Promised Land?

Reclaim God's Promised Blessings

Richard Everett

WHATEVER HAPPENED
TO THE PROMISED LAND?

ISBN: 978-1-8939581-2-8

Printed in the United States of America
All rights reserved under International Copyright Law

Published by:

GateKeeper Publishing, LLC
381 Casa Linda Plaza #406, Dallas, Texas 75218
www.gatekeeperpublishing.com

Cover design by April Campbell
GateKeeper Publishing, LLC

Library of Congress Cataloging-in-Publication Data

Everett, Richard

Whatever Happened to the Promised Land?
Reclaim God's Promised Blessings

ISBN: 978-1-8939581-2-8 (Paperback)
1. Personal Finance • Economics • Money Management

Unless otherwise indicated, all Scripture quotations are taken from the Amplified® Bible, Copyright © 1954, 1958, 1962, 1964, 1965, 1987 by The Lockman Foundation. Used by permission. (www.Lockman.org)

Additional Praise for the Book

"Biblical principles + Practical advice + Financial freedom = Opportunities to invest in Kingdom activity as a Steward of the Promised Land ... a must read for a blessed generation of believers."

––Dr. Stephen A. Macchia, President, Vision New England
Author, Becoming A Healthy Church

"The Promised Land symbolizes blessing, fruitfulness, abundant life, and prosperity – all things God desires for His children. Mr. Everett's book is practical, balanced, and workable. The financial principles he gives (if applied) will have a positive effect simply because it is God's Word."

––Rev. Floyd Miles, III
Teen Challenge International

Dedication

To my wife, MarySue, who has put up with me for 30 years. She is my partner in life and work, my spouse, lover, caretaker, best friend, business partner, and the "glue" that kept our family together through thick and thin with her prayers and faith. She's the Godliest woman I know.

To my daughter, my little princess, Jennifer: the nicest, kindest, sweetest, most caring young woman I know.

To my son, Shawn, the comic relief in our lives, growing every day towards his calling in life. His entrepreneurial spirit led him to sell his Easter candy door-to-door to our neighbors at age six so he could raise money to invest. May that spirit never die!

Acknowledgements

Reverend Thomson Mathew, my first pastor: He preached the first gospel message I ever heard. I have been heaven-bound ever since.

Pastor Bacon: He provided the nurturing guidance during a period in my life when I needed it the most.

Dave Cowan and Reverend Zeller: They both encouraged me to get into the financial field while I was $250,000 in debt. They obviously saw something I didn't.

Todd & Leslie Foster, my current pastors: I thank them for putting up with me.

Art Williams: He gave me a chance in the financial field when no one else would.

Attorney George Guertin for providing legal editing.

Sandra Woodbridge for providing accounting and tax editing.

Tricia Quinto for typing and providing grammatical editing.

Table of Contents

Chapter 1   My Story: Living in the Desert 15

Chapter 2   The Promised Land Revisited 19

Chapter 3   The Five Truths that Set Me Free 27

Chapter 4   The War on Poverty — Yours 43

Chapter 5   Stewardship 101 51

Chapter 6   Investing 101 71

Chapter 7   Financial Planning 101 97

Chapter 8   Final Thoughts — A Call to Action 125

Chapter 9   It's Not *WHAT* You Know,
It's *WHO* You Know 131

Chapter 10   Recommended Reading List
& Other Helpful Resources 135

Chapter 11   About the Author 141

Index of Basic Financial Terms 143

Chapter 1

My Story

My name is Richard Everett, and I run one of the nation's largest and most successful financial planning firms. "So what," you might say – "Big deal!" Considering where I came from and the financial disaster I went through, it is a big deal. In fact, it's a miracle!

In The Beginning

I was born in Columbus, Ohio in 1952. My parents divorced when I was very young. We barely made it financially. My mother did her best to raise my younger sister and me, while working countless hours just to pay the rent and put food on the table. We were poor, living in housing projects in the inner city. Eating pot pies and hamburgers was a luxury. My mother eventually remarried, and things got a little better. We always rented an apartment. Home ownership was never an option. We usually had just one automobile, and that was occasionally repossessed. Vacations were rare. You get the picture — we grew up in poverty.

We moved around quite a bit when I was a child. We lived in Florida, New Jersey, and Connecticut. I spent most of my adolescent years in New Haven, CT. It was the 1960s, and I wasn't very involved in sports or any other extracurricular activities. I was part of the "flower power" generation.

> We always rented ...ownership was never an option. We had just one automobile, and that was occasionally repossessed. You get the picture–we grew up in poverty.

After graduating from high school in 1970, I went to work in a factory. In 1975, I met my lovely wife-to-be, MarySue Delsanto. We were married the next year. Fortunately for both of us, we came to know Jesus Chris as our Lord and Saviour on our one-year wedding anniversary. We were both young and naïve when we got married. If we hadn't asked Jesus into our lives, I doubt our marriage would have lasted very long. Our beautiful daughter, Jennifer, was born in 1978, and our handsome son, Shawn, was born 18 months later.

A couple of years after our wedding, I decided to leave my factory job and start a career in sales. As a medical sales rep, I was often away on prolonged trips, which prevented me from experiencing the joys of watching our children grow up on a day-to-day basis. After much deliberation, we decided to start our own medical supply company. This allowed me to stay close to home and enjoy more time with our family. Unfortunately, our timing turned out to be horrible. Besides the financial strain of starting a new business, we hit one of the worse recessions the country had seen in years. The financial pressures, coupled with my lack of experience, forced us to close the business, lay off 30 people, and incur over $250,000 in debt. Our future looked bleak – no job, no savings, no income – just bills, lots of bills to pay. I was broke, unemployed, and had bill collectors breathing down my neck on a daily basis.

My Story – Living In the Desert

I needed a good paying job, and I needed it right away! Several friends and pastors suggested getting into the financial industry. Eventually, after much coaxing, I began a new career in the insurance and investments business. No salary – 100% commission. To say the least, I was motivated to succeed. You have to agree, God does have a sense of humor. A financial failure going into the financial planning business! The reality is, however, who would make a better financial planner than someone who has gone through a financial disaster? God has used failures throughout the old and new testaments to bring glory to His name – David, Peter, Moses, and Paul – to name a few. With God's help and direction, and through His Word, coupled with our hard work, focus and determination, we were able to get out of debt and become multi-millionaires in less than ten years!

Like most people, my life has been marked by setbacks, false starts and monetary difficulties. Through faith in God and His Word, especially principles dealing with finances and stewardship, I fashioned a lifestyle and mental discipline that allowed me, with God's help, to build the investment firm I run today.

My Own Firm

By 1987, I was doing well enough in the financial arena to go out on my own and establish the Everett Financial Group, Inc. Today, we have grown to become one of the area's largest and most respected independent financial planning firms. In the process, I have become well established in the financial industry. I am a Registered Financial Consultant (RFC), a Certified Senior Advisor (CSA), and member of the Financial Planning Association (FPA). I was named Financial Planner of the Year in 1996 by First Financial Planners, Inc., a national brokerage firm.

In addition to conducting hundreds of investment seminars throughout the Northeast, I have taught financial planning courses to municipal employees around the state, as well as at city libraries and various corporations. I have appeared numerous times on the local affiliate of ABC television and have hosted my own television and radio talk shows. Additionally, I have written numerous articles on financial planning and coauthored two books on investing and financial planning.

Whatever Happened to the Promised Land?

I have donated time to work with local churches and Sage Services (a United Way program) to help people in need of basic budgeting and financial counseling. In addition, I have had the privilege of serving on boards or committees of several non-profit organizations, including the Luis Palau Evangelistic Association, Teen Challenge, and Boy Scouts of America. I have offered my services because I have a lot of empathy for organizations and people who need help and guidance with money and finances. It can be hard finding professional financial counseling. This was one of the biggest problems we had during those difficult years when we earnestly wanted to put our financial house in order. The large brokerage firms had $25,000 minimums, which we didn't have. Banks and insurance companies were only interested in pushing products, not necessarily giving sound financial advice.

Coming from near bankruptcy to being president of a very successful financial planning firm, I know (without a shadow of a doubt) the Lord has called me to minister to the Christian community regarding God's stewardship principles. Without question, many Christians are hurting financially, and the need for sound, biblical financial counseling abounds. Unless we become the stewards He has designed us to be, we cannot receive the financial blessings the Lord intended for us. As a church, we must live a victorious life in all areas, including finances. With over 1,000 clients and over 150 million dollars under management, I believe I'm qualified to help people in financial need and to provide direction to those seeking to be financially free.

Success often rises out of the ashes of failure.

Whatever Happened to the Promised Land? offers conventional and biblical wisdom regarding money, finance, and stewardship and how we can apply these biblical lessons to everyday life, to live the abundant life the Word of God has promised. Many Christians have settled for a mediocre lifestyle and not the Promised Land, flowing with milk and honey. This book is a "road map to the Promised Land!" Who better to trust with our money and finances than God and His written Word?

The following chapters represent an accumulation of what I have learned over the past quarter century, both as a Christian businessman and a financial planner. My prayer is that these principles will bless you and your family as they have blessed us!

Chapter 2

The Promised Land Revisited

Whatever happened to the Promised Land? Let's take a look at the Bible and see what God intended for us. In Numbers 13:1, we read that the Lord said to Moses,

"Send some men to explore the land of Canaan, which I am giving to the Israelites."

Continuing with verse 17, when Moses sent them to explore Canaan, he said,

"Go up through the Negev and on into the hill country see what the land is like and whether the people who live there are strong or weak, few or many. What kind of land do they live in, is it good or bad? What kind of towns do they live in? Are they un walled or fortified? How is the soil, is it fertile or poor? Are there trees on it or not?"

Verses 26-33 go on to say,

"They came back to Moses and Aaron and the whole Israelite community in Kadesh in the desert of Paran. There they reported to them and to the whole assembly and showed them the fruit of the land."

They gave Moses this account,

"We went into the land to which you sent us and it does flow with milk and honey. Here are its fruits. But the people who live there are powerful and the cities are fortified and very large. We even saw Anak giants! The Amalekites live in the Negev and the Hittites and the Jebusites and the Amorites live in the hill country and the Canaanites live near the sea right along the Jordan. Then Caleb silenced the people before Moses and said, We should go up and take and possess the land, for we certainly can do it. But the men who had gone up with him said, we can't attack those people, they are stronger than we are and they spread among the Israelites a bad report about the land that they had explored. They said the land we explored devours those living in it. All the people we saw were of great size. We seem like grasshoppers in their eyes and we look the same to them."

Verse 1 of Chapter 14 continues,

"That night all the people of the community raised their voices and wept aloud. All the Israelites grumbled against Moses and Aaron."

Verses 6 & 7 of Chapter 14 go on to say,

"Joshua, son of Nun and Caleb, son of Jephunneh who were among those who had explored the land, tore their clothes and said to the entire Israelite assembly: The land we passed through and explored is exceedingly good. The Lord is pleased with us. He will lead us into the land. A land flowing with milk and honey."

Finally, in verse 23, God states,

> "Not one of them will ever see the land I promised on oath to their forefathers."

You are probably familiar with this story. Moses led the Israelites out of Egypt. God delivered them, brought them into the wilderness, and prepared them for the land that He had promised them for generations upon generations. As they were getting ready to go in, doubt and fear entered into the camp. As a consequence, they wandered the desert for 40 years, until finally entering in. It's a shame, because God had said, "Go into the land that I promised you." There was no reason for them not to enter in, and yet, because of doubt and unbelief, they wandered around the desert for four decades.

The Bible clearly states that God wants us to live in the Promised Land. He wants to bless us. He wants us to lead an abundant life, living in a land flowing with milk and honey. The Church of Jesus Christ has been going around for years, saying, "We're supposed to be poor. We're not supposed to be well off. Wealth is a sin or a sign of materialism." I do not find that in God's Word. I find just the opposite. Consider the following scriptures as proof that God wants us to enter in:

- *"Beloved, I wish above all things that thou mayest prosper. And be in health even as thy soul prospereth."* (III John verse 2)

- *"I have come that you might have life and have it more abundantly."* (John 10:10)

- *"Humility and the fear of the Lord brings wealth, honor and life."* (Proverbs 22:4)

- *"Blessed are all who fear the Lord and walk in His ways who will eat the fruit of your labor blessings and prosperity will be yours."* (Psalms 128:1,2)

- *"For you know the grace of our Lord, Jesus Christ that though He was rich yet for your sakes He became poor so that through His poverty you might become rich."* (II Corinthians 8:9)

Whatever Happened to the Promised Land?

- *"The blessings of the Lord bring wealth and He adds no trouble to it."* (Proverbs 10:22)

- *"Be strong and very courageous. Be careful to obey all the laws my servant Moses gave you. Do not turn from it to the right or to the left that you may be successful wherever you go. Do not let the Book of the Law depart from your mouth, meditate on it day and night so that you may be careful to do everything written in it. Then, you will be prosperous and successful."* (Joshua 1:7-9)

- *"I am the Lord thy God which teacheth thee to profit."* (Isaiah 48:17) This is one of my favorite scriptures.

- *"The God of heaven, He will prosper us."* (Nehemiah 2:20)

- *"The Lord God of your fathers make you a thousand times so many more as ye are, and bless you, as He hath promised you!"* (Deuteronomy 1:11)

- *"And He will love thee, and bless thee, and multiply thee: He will also bless the fruit of thy womb, and the fruit of thy land, thy corn, and thy wine, and thine oil. The increase of thy kin and the flocks of thy sheep, in the land which he sware unto thy fathers to give thee (the Promised Land). Thou shalt be blessed above all people."* (Deuteronomy 7:13, 14)

- *"Let the Lord be magnified, who has pleasure in the prosperity of His servant."* (Psalm 35:27)

- *"The Lord shall command the blessing upon thee in thy storehouse, and in all that thou settest thine hand unto; and he shall bless thee in the land which the Lord thy God giveth thee."* (Deuteronomy 28:8)

- *"Every man also to whom God hath given riches and wealth, and hath given him power to eat thereof, and to take his portion, and to rejoice in his labor: this is a gift from God."* (Ecclesiastes 5:19)

- *"But thou shalt remember the Lord thy God: for it is he that giveth thee power to get wealth, that he may establish his covenant which he sware unto thy fathers, as it is this day."* (Deuteronomy 8:18)

- *"And Jabez called on the God of Israel saying, 'Oh, that you would bless me indeed, and enlarge my territory, that your hand would be with me, and that you would keep me from evil, that I may not cause pain!' So God granted him what he requested."* (I Chronicles 4:10)

• *"Praise the Lord! Blessed is the man who fears the Lord, who delights greatly in His commandments. His descendants will be mighty on earth; the generation of the upright will be blessed. Wealth and riches will be in his house, and his righteousness endures forever."* (Psalm 112:1-3)

Any Questions?

From Genesis to Revelation, it's very clear that God wants to bless us –– His chosen people –– and yet (just like the Israelites), we wander in the desert. Think about the people throughout the Bible whom God has blessed –– Adam and Eve, Abraham, Isaac, Jacob, David, Solomon, Joseph of Aramathea, and Job. They were all wealthy. They had it all. (Even Noah was rich. His stock was rising while everyone else's was in liquidation!) There are those throughout the Bible whom God had chosen to bless. He wants to do the same thing for all of us –– those who are His chosen, the followers of God in Christ.

This is not a "name it and claim it," "blab it or grab it" message. Those messages went around in the 70's and 80's and got people nowhere.

This is not a "name it and claim it," "blab it or grab it" message. Those messages went around in the 70s and 80s and got people nowhere. This is, however, an economic empowerment message, because God does want to empower us economically so that we can do things for Him in this life, not only in our communities but around the world. In God's Word, you'll discover most of His promises addressing wealth and prosperity are conditional upon obedience to His Word. If God does want us to live in the Promised Land, my questions are — Why is the Church of Jesus Christ in such a financial bind? Why are the Saints of God, the body of Christ, up to their ears in debt, living paycheck to paycheck, barely making ends meet? (Making ends meet means you are running in circles.)

Frankly, we are a poor testimony to the world. When an unbeliever sees us struggling financially, don't they think or say, "I don't want to be like them. Look at them struggling." "What's so special about being a Christian?" To be quite candid, many Christians are horrible examples to the unsaved. It's not altogether their fault though. Unfortunately, the church is conspicuously silent on the subject of money. Once in a while, we hear a sermon on tithing or giving, usually when there is a building project or a special offering — a little self-serving, I would say. Since most ministers have taken a vow of poverty (whether self-imposed or church board-imposed), rarely is an impoverished person qualified to give good, sound advice on the subject of money, finance, and stewardship. "And the beat goes on," generation after generation of financial illiterates. The church, unfortunately, has rarely been a good source of information on economic empowerment.

While I'm on the subject, allow me to get on my "soap box." The lack of financial education in our homes, schools, and churches really bothers me. Where is someone just starting out in life supposed to learn about how to use money? In my younger days, I used to coach a Bible quiz team in our church. It was a great program. Each year, our team would memorize a book in the Bible and compete against

What kind of message are we teaching our children?

other churches. It was similar to the game show Jeopardy but with teams. It was both intense and fun! While visiting another church to compete in a tournament, I noticed a scripture posted in one of the Sunday school rooms. It read, "Money is the root of all evil." This still bothers me years later. I Timothy 6:10 states, "For the *love* of money is the root of all evil," not money! I can't tell you how many times I hear that verse misquoted, and it burns me up. What kind of message are we teaching our young people? Money is not evil. Money is neither good nor evil. It's a tool, like the television. The Gospel message can be seen, but, unfortunately, so can pornography, depending on the viewer. In the hands of a good person, money is used for good purposes. In the hands of a bad person, money is used for bad purposes. Why would anyone teach our young people that money is evil? Remember, Jesus had a treasurer. It was Judas' love of money that was his downfall, not the money itself.

The Promised Land Revisited

I remember taking all kinds of courses in junior and senior high school, subjects such as geology, biology, and earth science. I have nothing against these subjects, but the reality is — how many people become biologists or geologists? Not many! On the other hand, I don't remember any classes on balancing a checkbook, operating within a budget, or basic investing. This is probably because most teachers were not taught these basics when they were in school. Why aren't these important subjects addressed in the classroom? Every graduate is forced to deal with money on a daily basis. The vicious cycle continues, generation after generation! (Okay, I'm off my "soap box" now. Let's take a look at the Israelites' plight.)

Why didn't the Israelites enter into the Promised Land? Three reasons…

1. Lack of knowledge
2. Unbelief
3. Lack of action

- Hosea 4:6 says, *"My people are destroyed due to lack of knowledge."* Many of us don't know how to handle money, finances, or how to be good stewards.

- Hebrews 3:19 clearly says, *"They did not enter in* (talking about the Israelites) *due to their unbelief."*

- In Deuteronomy 1:26, God says to the Israelites, *"but you were unwilling."*

> Failure will never overtake you if your determination to succeed is strong enough.

What's keeping you out of the Promised Land?

- John 10:10 says, *"The thief cometh only to steal, kill and destroy."*

I read that verse for years, and I didn't realize for a long time that the key word in that scripture is "only." Satan has an agenda. He is here for three reasons — to *steal* your Promised Land, to *kill* you, and to *destroy* you and your family.

The good news is that Jesus said in John 8:32, "you shall know the truth and the truth shall set you free." God's Word is truth (John 17:17), and the truths found in His word are liberating.

Whatever Happened to the Promised Land?

Just over 20 years ago, we were broke. (In fact, I was so broke, I couldn't even pay attention.) We were a quarter of a million dollars in debt. Inflated to today's dollars, that's about one million dollars. That's a lot of money! We had no savings, were "up to our ears" in debt and had no hope; the future looked bleak. (As a matter of fact, I came from a long line of business failures. My grandfather invented one of those change machines where you put in a dollar and get four quarters. He couldn't make a profit either.)

Quite frankly, times were desperate back then. We literally came to a point where we didn't have food to feed our children. I am not exaggerating. The lowest point of my life as a husband and father was the day my wife asked me what we were going to feed our children that evening. We had absolutely nothing left. I turned away from my wife, so she wouldn't see me cry, and said, "The Lord will provide." I firmly believed He would but didn't know how. Hours later, a complete stranger showed up at our front door and handed me a one hundred dollar bill. He simply said that God had instructed him to do so — and left. Please remember, 20 years ago, one hundred dollars bought a month's worth of groceries. I call that a miracle! Twice during those difficult times, bags of groceries mysteriously showed up on our front steps. God is always on time! Fortunately, friends and pastors began to share Godly financial advice with my wife and me. We had thought money was an unholy and ungodly thing and that God didn't have anything to say about it. With renewed excitement, we began to search the scriptures for help and hope. We found that He, indeed, has a lot to say about finances and stewardship. Once we began to apply these "truths" to our lives, things began to change for the better.

Chapter Three focuses on five truths that set our family financially free. Read on and enter in!

Chapter 3

The Five Truths That Set Me Free

There are five truths that made a huge difference in our lives, the truths God used to take us from financial ruin and humiliation to financial freedom, from the pit to the Promised Land. Clearly, God has a game plan for us on how to be a good steward and how to live a blessed and abundant life. There is, indeed, a road map in the Bible that shows how to find the Promised Land — very clear directions on how to enter in!

Truth #1 — God is A Giver

- John 3:16 states, *"God so loved the world that He gave His only begotten son. That whosoever believe in Him should not perish, but have everlasting life."*

- Hebrews 2:4 says, *"God also bearing them witness both with signs and wonders with diverse miracles, and gifts of the Holy Ghost, according to His will."*

- Romans 8:32 says, *"He spared not His own son, but delivered Him up for us. How shall He not with Him also give us freely all things."*

- Finally, John 17:2 states, *"As thou has given Him power over all flesh, that He should give eternal life to as many as thou hast given Him."* Think about what God has given you! Frankly, that's amazing grace.

Earn All You Can. Save All You Can. Give All You Can.
–John Wesley

Truth #2 — He wants us to be givers.

Because God, by His very nature, is a giver, He wants us to be like Him and be givers. Luke 6:38 says, *"Give, and it shall be given."* Most of us are familiar with that scripture. We have probably heard it dozens of times, but that scripture goes on to say, *"Good measure pressed down, shaken together, running over, shall men give onto your bosom."* Here is the catch — *"For the same measure that you use will be used back to you."* Let that sink in before you continue. If you give a little, you get a little. What measure are you using — a shot glass or a wheelbarrow? II Corinthians 9:10,11 states,

> "He who supplies seed to the sower and bread for food will supply and multiply your resources and increase the harvest of your righteousness. You will be enriched in every way for great generosity, which through us will produce thanksgiving to God..."

Many of the stories in the Bible are based on farming because that was the primary "industry" of the day. It was something the people of that time could relate to. The above scripture says, *"Now He (God) who supplied seed to the sower ..."* Why would God give seed to someone who doesn't sow or to someone who wastes the seed? God is looking for vessels, human beings who He can use to give seeds, so they can plant, sow, and multiply them. He is not looking for people who are going to take the seeds, throw them in a drawer, and not do anything with them. God gives seeds to the sower, not to those who waste. If you are a sower, then God can give you more. He is in the multiplication business. He also expects us to multiply what He gives us. What a great illustration!

In II Corinthians 9:6, Paul states, *"Whoever sows sparingly, reaps sparingly."* (Again talking in terms of agriculture.) If you had to feed your family, and you had a barrel full of seeds, would you plant a few seeds or plant them all? What kind of harvest are you planting? If you plant only a few seeds, you are going to starve to death. The same thing is true with God's principles of giving. If you give a little, then you will reap little also. Those who sow abundantly will also reap an abundant harvest. Have you ever known a successful farmer who just planted a few seeds and didn't work hard? (I haven't either.) In Galatians, Paul states, *"God is not mocked: For whatsoever a man soweth, that shall he also reap."*

One of my favorite stories in the Bible is found in I Samuel 1:27-28. It's the story of Hannah, who tried for years to conceive a child. She went into the temple, prayed, and God answered her prayer. She responded to God, *"I prayed for this child and the Lord has granted me what I have asked of Him, so now I will give him back to the Lord."* Because she gave back the most precious thing in her life – her first born son – the Lord was gracious to Hannah. She later gave birth to three sons and two daughters (a five-fold increase). Her first son, Samuel, grew up in the presence of the Lord and became a great man of God.

"Freely you have received, freely give." (Matthew 10:8)

Beware — we shouldn't give just to get! Our motives for giving should be pure. Ananias and Sapphira (Acts Chapter 5) gave, but they died because their motives were not pure. Remember — *"God loves a cheerful giver"* (II Cor. 9:7). I firmly believe that everything that we have is from God. We are His stewards, and He wants to use us to distribute His wealth as needs and opportunities arise. It's the law of reciprocity — the more you give, the more you receive.

I love reading biographies and autobiographies of very wealthy people. I am interested in how they made it and how they handled it. There is a common thread among many of the ultra wealthy. John D. Rockefeller, one of the first billionaires in the world, tithed at age 19 while making only $25/month. When he became a millionaire, then a multi-millionaire, and then a billionaire, he always understood that the money he made was not his. He was a Christian and was brought up in a very devout Baptist home. He continually understood that he was just a conduit that God used to make money flow through. This is what Mr. Rockefeller had to say about money:

> "I believe the power to make money is a gift from God — just as are the instincts for art, music, literature, the doctor's talent, the nurse's, yours –– to be developed and used to the best of our ability for the good of mankind. Having been endowed with the gift I possess, I believe it is my duty to make money and still more money, and to use the money I make for the good of my fellow man according to the dictates of my conscience."

Many other wealthy individuals, such as J.C. Penney, Andrew Carnegie, Joan Kroc (the wife of the founder of McDonald's Corp.), and Bill Gates of Microsoft, also understood their duty to give. They have given away billions to help others.

"To whom much is given, much is required." Luke 12:48.

Wealth Is Good If It Is Used To Bring Joy To Others

Here are six good reasons to give:

1. Proverbs 10:16 tells us that our paychecks and our earnings should be used to further the righteous causes, to help build churches and to help in ministry. It says, "A good man's earnings advance the cause of righteousness." That speaks for itself.

2. Proverbs 22:9 is one of the many scriptures that talks about the poor. *"Happy is the generous man who feeds the poor."* If you're miserable, you know why.

3. Proverbs 28:27, *"If you give to the poor, your needs will be supplied, but a curse upon those who close their eyes to poverty."*

4. Proverbs 14:21 *"To despise the poor is sin, but blessed are those who pity them."* (It can't get any clearer than that.)

5. Proverbs 21:13 *"He who shuts his ears to the cries of the poor will be ignored in his own time of need."* Will you have a time of need?

6. Proverbs 19:17 (one of my favorites) *"When you help the poor, you are lending to the Lord – and He pays wonderful interest on your loan."* What are the banks guaranteeing these days? What is God guaranteeing? When you help the poor, you're lending to the Lord and He pays wonderful interest on the loan! Think about that.

God Is More Interested In Your Standard of Giving Than Your Standard of Living.
–Rev. Calvin Bacon

Proverbs 11:24 and 25 tells us that the more we give, the more we receive. It says, *"It is possible to give away and become richer."* It doesn't make any sense in the world's eyes, but the Word says it is possible to give away and become richer. If God said it, I believe it. *"It is also possible to hold on too tightly and to lose everything."* If you can be found faithful with $100, He can entrust you with $1,000. If you can be faithful with $1,000, then He can give you $10,000. There is no limit to what God can do. It's possible to give away and become richer. If we hoard it, then God can't and won't use us. *"Yes, the liberal man shall be rich: by watering others he shall water himself."*

In the parable of the rich fool (Luke 12:20-21), God said to the greedy individual, *"You fool! This very night your life will be demanded from you. Then who will get what you have prepared for yourself? This is how it will be with anyone who stores up things for himself but is not rich toward God."*

Acts 20:35 says, *"It is more blessed to give than to receive."* Is it more blessed to give than it is to receive? As parents, we all experience the joy of giving at Christmas time. My joy at Christmas was watching our young children open their presents. When my wife and I were first saved, we made it a practice every Christmas to anonymously give to those that were in need at our church. (I believe anonymously is the way it should be done. The Lord says, when you are giving, *"don't let the left hand know what the right hand is doing."* He also says if you want praise from men, then that's all you're going to get. I prefer to please God. Back to my story...)

So, each December we would give our pastor $500 to distribute among those who needed it the most. I remember the first year we did it. My wife dropped me off at the church. She was going to run a few errands, then come back to pick me up. I went in to see the pastor and gave him the money. While I was waiting in the foyer for my wife to pick me up, a woman from the church came in for an appointment with the pastor. I was still waiting when she came out again. It was one of the most amazing things I had ever seen. She had the glow of an angel. I said, "What's the matter? What's going on?" She replied, "Rich, you

Giving is the key to receiving.

have no idea what God has just done for us." (Her husband was an alcoholic. He deserted her and her three girls years earlier. She was living at the poverty level.) "I didn't have a penny for Christmas, but God just blessed me. I'm able to buy clothes and toys for my three daughters." I was able to witness firsthand how indeed it is more blessed to give! Seeing the joy on her face gave me so much joy that Christmas, especially since she did not know it was from us. Giving is the key to receiving!

Acts 10:4 tells us that God notices giving. The scriptures say, "And the angel replied," (talking to Cornelius, the first Gentile household to receive the Holy Spirit) "Your prayers and charities have not gone unnoticed by God."

Our giving should be from a pure heart, and our motives should be honorable. Remember Ananias and Sapphira. God is not our magic genie or Santa Claus. We shouldn't give for the wrong reasons. If you implement these giving principles in your life, God will bless you more than you can ever ask or think. God honors His Word. One of the highest compliments I ever received was from my pastor, when he said to me, "Richard, you are one of the few people to figure it out. You gave your way out of financial ruin. I believe that's the reason God has blessed your family with abundance."

Can't afford to give? Read the following story found in Mark 12:41-44, and see if you still feel the same way:

Then He (Jesus) went over to the collection boxes in the Temple and sat and watched as the crowds dropped in their money. Some who were rich put in large amounts. Then a poor widow came and dropped in two pennies. He called His disciples to Him and remarked, "That poor widow has given more than all those rich men put together! For they gave a little of their surplus, while she gave up her last penny."

Is your lack of giving keeping you out of the Promised Land?

Money Does Little For The Soul, Until You Give It Away.
–Rev. Robert Schuller

Truth 3 — Tithing is not an option.

Tithing is not an option, particularly if you want to make it into the Promised Land. Many Christians are in denial (not a river in Egypt) about tithing. I do a fair amount of financial counseling. Many pastors send me people who are having financial difficulties. The first thing I ask in our sessions is, "Do you tithe?" Almost always, the answer is "no." I firmly believe this is the major reason they are having financial difficulties in the first place. They give me all kinds of excuses —"Well, that was part of the law. That wasn't part of the new covenant. Jesus never said anything about tithing." Really? Not according to my Bible!

Briefly, let's take a look at what God has to say about tithing. In Genesis 14:18-20, it is very simply stated, "Abraham tithed to Melchizedek." Melchizedek was the High Priest at the time. Abraham was around before the law was given. Tithing probably goes back to Adam and Eve and was passed along from generation to generation. Cain and Abel gave an offering way back in the beginning. So, tithing predates "the law."

Whatever Happened to the Promised Land?

Want to know what Jesus said about tithing? In Matthew 23:23, Jesus said, "Yes, you should tithe" (Living Bible — red letter edition). If Jesus said it, it's part of the new covenant, post law. There is also a passage of scripture I am sure you have heard many times; nevertheless, I want to dwell on it for a few minutes. It's Malachi 3:8-11; God is speaking,

"Will a man rob God, yet you rob me. But you ask, how do we rob you? In tithes and offerings. You're under a curse. The whole nation of you, because you are robbing me. Bring the whole tithe, into the storehouse, that food may be found in my house. Test me in this, says the Lord God Almighty, and see if I will not open the floodgates of heaven and pour out so much blessing that you will not have room enough for it. I will rebuke the devourer for your sakes."

That's an incredible scripture, containing so many truths! You could write an entire book just on those four verses. There are so many things that God wants us to understand. First of all, He says the whole tithe. The "tithe" simply is a word meaning ten, one-tenth, 10% –– not 9%, 5%, or 0%. He says bring the whole tithe or 10% into the storehouse, into the church of God. God says, "You rob me." In other words, we are thieves if we don't tithe. It's that simple. If you had children who were stealing from you, how would you respond? Would you look the other way or would you punish them? What do you think our Heavenly Father will do? Although He is not an ogre, it is very clear that He wants us tithe. It's a required act of obedience. Remember — it's a tithe, not a tip!

The Lord went on to say, "You're cursed with a curse." Your 100% can't possibly go as far as God's 90%. God makes everything stretch. I see it all the time. God wants to bless you, but there's just one little condition — give back ten percent. He said "if you can't trust me when it comes to money, then I can't bless you". The Lord also said, "Test me." It's the only time that I know of in the Bible where God actually says, "Test me." What does God want with your money anyway? He is the creator of everything. What good is money to God? It's a test, to see if you can trust Him!

Why is it we can trust God with our very soul, our salvation, and our eternity, but we can't trust Him regarding money? It doesn't make sense to me. Why is it we can bless the mall and not bless our Maker? According to Malachi 1:14, God doesn't want our leftovers either. If you read the whole story in the first chapter of Malachi, God is a little upset. He says, "Cursed is the cheat who has an acceptable male in his flock and vows to give it, and then sacrifices a blemished animal to the Lord." You know the law is very clear on what the Israelites were to sacrifice. It was the first fruit, the one without blemish. Do you know what they were doing in Malachi's day? They were promising or vowing to give their best and then giving God their junk. God was not happy.

The Bible says quite clearly, *"Cursed is the cheat."* No one wants to be cursed by God. (This is where I tick off everyone.) According to Leviticus 27:31, if a man redeems any of his tithe, he must add one-fifth or 20% to its value. Clearly, it states there is a 20% penalty for not paying your tithe on time. Let me make something clear. It's not our job, ministry, or "spiritual gift" to determine how God's tithe is to be used. If we do that, then we begin to play God. Frankly, it's not our tithe; it's His tithe.

Allow me to share a true story. It's one of the few success stories I have from dozens of counseling sessions. The reason this is one of the few success stories is that most people having financial problems don't want to talk about or deal with tithing. They don't understand that not tithing may be the primary reason for their financial difficulties. So, they wander in the desert for 40 years! Too bad! Like the Israelites before them, it didn't have to happen!

A number of years ago, my pastor referred a young couple to me, John & Mary, who had three small children. At our first meeting, Mary started to cry. While sobbing, she said, "Richard, we're in debt up to our ears. We can barely make ends meet. I can't go to work, because I have to stay home and take care of the kids. John only works 35 hours a week, his employer doesn't offer any overtime, and we can't find any part-time work." As I gave her a box of tissues, I asked Mary, "How much debt do you have?" She answered, "Well ... $3,000." I replied, "I was a quarter of a million dollars in debt. I probably can help you. I can give you some guidance and directions on getting out of debt. But I have to ask this question. (It is the first question I always ask in counseling sessions.) "Are you tithing?" They looked at each other, and then she said, "Well, sort of." (Tithing is like being pregnant — either you are or you aren't. You can't "sort of" tithe, just like you can't "sort of" be pregnant.) So I said, "I'll tell you what — we'll stop right now. The two of you go home and discuss whether or not you want to put God first in the area of your finances and if you're willing to start tithing. You can come back, and I'll put together a plan for you. I'll show you how to get out of debt. It might take two years; it might take five years, but if the two of you decide to put God first in the area of finances, God will honor your decision. You will see things begin to get better. I can't say how He will do it, but He will. God always honors His word!"

She called me back early the next morning. "We talked it over. We're going to tithe; we'll put God first." I showed them how to put a budget and a financial plan together, and they promised to work on it together. I said to them, "You know God's Word is always true. He will bless you. Period. It may not be this week; it may not be this year, but He will do it. He will help you get out of debt as long as you're faithful."

Well, Mary called me back about two weeks later and said, "Richard, you're not going to believe this. John just got notice that he will be forced to work 50 hours per week for the next two years. His company just received a large contract. We're going to take that overtime money and apply it towards our debt." She said, "You were right. God is faithful." About two or three weeks later, she called me again and said, "Richard, you're not going to believe this." (Remember, she's a young woman with three children. She couldn't go out to work but periodically held Tupperware parties. She hadn't held a Tupperware party in six months because the economy was so horrible.) "I have already booked six Tupperware parties for next month! We're going to take all that extra money and apply it towards our debt."

About a week or two later, I received another call from Mary. She said, "Richard, you are not going to believe this. We have missionary friends, who own a home in a nearby town. They are going to China to minister for two years. They want us to live in their house — free. All we have to do is pay the utilities for the two years they are away." (Mary and John didn't own a house but rented.) "By the way, our lease is up at the same time." (What a coincidence!) They moved into the house, lived there practically for free, only paying utilities. Once they moved into their rent-free home, their new next door neighbor asked if Mary could take care of her young child, since Mary was home all day with her own kids. This resulted in an additional $200 per month for John and Mary.

We lost contact with them shortly after they moved out of town and started to attend another church. About 12-18 months later, my wife saw Mary at a grocery store. Mary said, "Tell Richard he's not going to believe this. With John's overtime, money from Tupperware parties, not having to pay rent, and the extra baby-sitting money, we are now completely, 100% debt-free and have saved enough for a down payment on a new home."

That's a true story. Unfortunately, as I stated earlier, it's one of my few success stories. Nearly everyone else who has come to me for counseling has never come back after I challenged them to tithe and put God first in their finances. There are 38 references to tithing in the Bible. Ignore them at your own risk. Entering into the Promised Land is a choice — so is wandering in the desert.

Is your lack of tithing keeping you out of the Promised Land?

Truth #4 — God wants us to properly manage what He gives us.

God wants us to be planners, stewards and excellent managers of what He gives us. Here's proof,

> Proverbs 21:5 says, "The plans of the diligent lead to profit" In other words, you have to be diligent with putting a plan together for your family, developing a budget, and setting goals in your household.

Tony, a friend from church, approached me a couple of years ago. He wanted me to review his business plan. Frankly, he is the only Christian I know who took the time to write a business plan. God is blessing him! He will bless you too, if you take the time to plan properly. I know too many people who went out and started a business without any written plan, goals, or budget. They ended up going out of business, bitter and broke. They blamed others instead of looking in the mirror. Develop a written plan for your life, set goals, and stay focused.

If you really want to do something, you'll find a way; if you don't, you'll find an excuse.

Romans 12:11 says, *"Do not be slothful in business."*

Unfortunately, I see it all the time, particularly with Christian business people. They pay people "under the table," are paid "under the table," do all kinds of immoral or illegal things, and then try to justify it. God blesses those who are honest and upright. Remember to stand up for what is right, don't be slothful in business, and have integrity. What is integrity? It's doing the right thing even when no one is looking.

Luke 16:10 says, *"Whoever can be trusted with very little can also be trusted with much."* Think about it. How much are you being entrusted with? Whoever is dishonest with very little will also be dishonest with much. Be honest with everything; have integrity in everything that you do.

Here's another short story. A number of years ago, my wife and I took our children to Disney World. We flew down to Florida, rented a car, and stayed at a hotel near the park. (Don't ever go on vacation with me. If you do, it'll rain, and you'll have to do it my way and stay on a strict time schedule. I have an agenda from 8 o'clock in the morning to 10 o'clock at night.) The next morning, I was in a hurry to get to Disney World. Unfortunately, there was a line to pay for parking.

The parking attendants collect the money on both the passenger side and on the driver's side of the car. My wife gave the attendant a $100 bill. We didn't count the change right away. I assumed it was correct and drove off. My wife turned to me and said, "They gave us a hundred and ten dollars change, instead of the $90 we were supposed to get back.." ("Not bad," some people would say. Or, "Praise the Lord.")

I said to myself, *I have to get to Space Mountain by 9 AM.* (You should always do the right thing, because the Word says that he who can be trusted with little can be trusted with a lot. Besides, my kids were watching!)

Ever try giving money back to somebody? You get the strangest looks. Trying to give money back at Disney World was not easy! We owed them twenty dollars. We immediately got into the park and asked for the location of the office. The employee said, "What's the problem?" I said, "I want to give some money back. The parking attendant gave us too much change." (The looks were unbelievable!) After several attempts, we found the office and spoke to a clerk. She asked, "So what's the problem?"

"The problem is — we want to give you twenty dollars back; you gave us too much change."

"What? They didn't give you enough change?"

Finally, we were able to give the money back. That poor girl at the parking lot who gave us the incorrect change would have had to make it up out of her own pocket. Keeping the money was not the right thing to do; it was not my money.

The interesting thing about this story is that I never gave it a second thought until we boarded the plane after the vacation was over. Because we did the right thing, three blessings took place on that vacation that I initially took for granted. The first blessing was that we were upgraded to a suite instead of the normal hotel room we had reserved. (We didn't put up much of a fight.) Secondly, on one of the nights we went out to eat, we were given free desserts and coffee because the service was a little slow. Thirdly, on another night, the service was even slower. We were told, "I'm sorry it took so long. Your whole dinner is free." "Whoever can be trusted with a little can be trusted with much (Luke 16:10)." Thank God for his faithfulness — and free dessert!

Is your lack of stewardship keeping you out of the Promised Land?

Truth #5 — Financial freedom won't be easy, but it will be worth it!

Genesis 3:17 and 19 say, *"Cursed is the ground because of you. Through painful toil you will eat of it all the days of your life."* Not some of the days, but all of the days of your life. "And by the sweat of your brow, you will eat your food until you return to the ground." Nothing in this life is easy. The journey will be tough; it is part of the curse. Anything worthwhile in this life will take hard work, determination and commitment, whether it's having a successful marriage, parenting, fostering a harmonious family life, or building a church or a business. As Ringo Starr said, "It don't come easy." Life is rough. So what! Get over it. We won't be here forever. The difference between somebody winning in life and losing in life is not quitting. Someone famous once said, "Ninety percent of winning is just showing up." Isn't that the truth! Most people just don't "show up." "Stuff" happens to everybody. It's a test. "F" or "A" — it's your choice.

Be strong — and work; for I am with you, says the Lord. (Haggai 2:4)

Whatever Happened to the Promised Land?

Let's get back to the Israelites in the desert. They were sitting in their tents grumbling for the better part of 40 years, until they finally entered into the Promised Land. When they entered in, they still had many battles to fight. The same thing is true for us. If you want to enter your Promised Land (your destiny), you will have battles to fight. God will go ahead of you, and He will help you win the victory. He will give you the required strength. He will even fight some of the battles for you. Quitters won't make it. Remember, winners never quit, and quitters never win! After all, most good and worthwhile things take time to achieve. You don't wake up one morning and decide to enter the Olympics. It takes training, conditioning, and focus. If you decide to have a child, you have to wait nine full months. You don't have a baby overnight. Rome wasn't built in a day. Financial independence takes time. As Winston Churchill said, "Never give up, never give up, never give up."

It's Always Too Soon To Give Up

Here's one final story before I end this chapter. My pastor was preaching a series called "God and... " on God and Your Money, God and Your Prayers, etc. After the sermon on "God and Your Money," at least 200 people went to the altar for prayer regarding their financial needs. A couple of weeks later, a guest speaker came to our church and preached a message on economic empowerment for the church and its people. It was a mid-week service, and there were no more than 150 people in attendance. I counted at least 100 at the altar for prayer at the end of the service. Our church also has a class on financial freedom, how to get out of debt, how to become economically empowered, etc. I don't mean for this to sound condemning, but, the last time the class was held, only one person attended. I don't get it! Hundreds of people come to the altar for a five-minute prayer for their financial problems and then go home and don't change. What are they expecting—that God will somehow deposit one million dollars into their bank accounts? Most people are looking for the easy way out — "God, *You* do it!"

> Hundreds come to the altar for a **five-minute prayer** for their financial problems and then go home and **don't change.**

How can God turn our finances around, unless we take the first step and make the effort? What do we expect from a five-minute prayer– for Santa Claus to come down the chimney with a large bag of money? It doesn't happen that way. Unless we change, live by God's Word, live within our means, get out of debt, do the right things, and educate ourselves, He cannot bless us the way He truly wants to. We have to change first. It's a choice. Going to the Promised Land is a choice. I hate to break this to you, but there is no Santa Claus. Although unfortunately, we treat God that way sometimes. We send up a short prayer about what we need and then expect Him to arrive the next day with our toy. It doesn't work that way. How many people do you know who have become financially independent by sending up a five-minute prayer? I don't know any either. Getting to the Promised Land (financial freedom) is hard, but it's worth it!

Is laziness, lack of focus, or lack of discipline keeping you from entering the Promised Land? The fact of the matter is the Israelites sat, as I said earlier, in their tents and grumbled. I think they expected God to go out and fight the battles and let them just cross over. Are we sitting in our homes, grumbling against God, expecting him to deliver us from our financial problems and bondage, when we haven't even lifted a finger to change our current economic condition? How can God bless us with the abundance He truly wants us to have, unless we take the first step?

Courage Is Being Scared To Death, But Going Forward Anyway !

Chapter 4

The War On Poverty –Yours

Would you like to be involved in the war on poverty — your poverty? In order to help you fight that war, allow me to share seven ideas on how to get your money working for you instead of you working for it. Achieving financial success is not impossible. It takes hard work (sorry that I keep bringing up that four- letter word), focus, determination, and sacrifice. "Sacrifice," you say. "I don't want to do that." Then stay poor. I found out a long time ago that it was easier to become a good steward than to continue to make excuses. Here is the "ammunition" that will help you win the war.

1. Take advantage of "free" money. Not too long ago, I had a meeting with a young woman. She wanted to start an investment

plan but didn't have any money to get started. She had access to her company's 401(k) retirement plan, but she was not contributing to the plan, even though her company matched fifty cents on the dollar. What a shame! Free money is normally a good thing! The more I delved into her financial situation, I discovered she would stop at Starbucks for a café latte on her way to work each day. I wasn't sure what that was, since I don't drink coffee. I asked, "How much do they cost?" She answered, "Three dollars." I asked, "Why don't you buy yourself a can of coffee, make your own coffee in the morning, and take the three bucks a day and put it in your 401(k)?" Remember — her company would add fifty cents to every dollar she contributed. That's four and one-half dollars per day, times five days a week, times 52 weeks a year, which totals $1,125 per year. Invested at 12% (hypothetical investment return, just shy of the stock market average over the last 104 years), for 40 years (retiring at 65) – do you have any idea what that will be worth? It's worth just shy of one million dollars — $966,000 to be exact! She had no idea how expensive café latte really was.

So, when I hear people say, "I don't have any money to invest," generally it's a matter of priority, not a lack of finances. If you knew you could be a millionaire by giving up coffee, would you?

2. Prioritize. What is more important to you — financial freedom or wandering in the wilderness? My junior high school teacher did an eye-opening exercise way back in the olden days, illustrating the true cost of smoking cigarettes over a long period of time. Back then, cigarettes were fifty cents per pack. Allow me to share this illustration with you at current prices. Let's say you are 40 years old and smoke a pack a day. Multiply five dollars a day (the estimated average cost of a pack of cigarettes over the next 25 years) by 365 days. That's $1,825 per year. A 40-year-old investing that amount at a hypothetical 12% for 25 years (you'll probably now live another 25 years because you gave up smoking), comes to $272,000 – over a quarter of a million dollars! (Although the cigarette does the smoking, it still requires a sucker on the end.) If you don't smoke, then what about giving up cable TV, a meal, a second phone line, a water cooler, or how about just sacrificing something to be able to become financially free and live where God wants you to live? The Promised Land!

3. Understand the time value of money. The sooner you start, the easier it is to accumulate wealth. "Early Bloomer Bob" starts investing $2,000 at a 12% hypothetical rate of return at age twenty-two, for six years and stops investing. "Peter Procrastinator" spends $2,000 a year on himself for six years and then decides to invest $2,000 at 12%. Mr. Procrastinator must invest $2,000 a year for 35 years to catch Mr. Early Bloomer.

Age	Early Bloomer Bob		Peter Procrastinator	
	Payment	Year End Accumulation	Payment	Year End Accumulation
22	$ 2,000	$ 2,240	$ 0	$ 0
23	$ 2,000	$ 4,749	$ 0	$ 0
24	$ 2,000	$ 7,559	$ 0	$ 0
25	$ 2,000	$ 10,706	$ 0	$ 0
26	$ 2,000	$ 14,230	$ 0	$ 0
27	$ 2,000	$ 18,178	$ 0	$ 0
28	$ 0	$ 20,359	$ 2,000	$ 2,240
29	$ 0	$ 22,803	$ 2,000	$ 4,749
30	$ 0	$ 25,539	$ 2,000	$ 7,559
31	$ 0	$ 28,603	$ 2,000	$ 10,706
32	$ 0	$ 32,036	$ 2,000	$ 14,230
33	$ 0	$ 35,880	$ 2,000	$ 18,178
34	$ 0	$ 40,186	$ 2,000	$ 22,559
35	$ 0	$ 45,008	$ 2,000	$ 27,551
36	$ 0	$ 50,409	$ 2,000	$ 33,097
37	$ 0	$ 56,458	$ 2,000	$ 39,309
38	$ 0	$ 63,233	$ 2,000	$ 46,266
39	$ 0	$ 70,821	$ 2,000	$ 54,058
40	$ 0	$ 79,320	$ 2,000	$ 62,785
41	$ 0	$ 88,838	$ 2,000	$ 72,559
42	$ 0	$ 99,499	$ 2,000	$ 83,507
43	$ 0	$ 111,438	$ 2,000	$ 95,767

Whatever Happened to the Promised Land?

Age	Early Bloomer Bob		Peter Procrastinator	
	Payment	Year End Accumulation	Payment	Year End Accumulation
44	$ 0	$ 124,811	$ 2,000	$ 109,499
45	$ 0	$ 139,788	$ 2,000	$ 124,879
46	$ 0	$ 156,563	$ 2,000	$ 142,105
47	$ 0	$ 175,351	$ 2,000	$ 161,397
48	$ 0	$ 196,393	$ 2,000	$ 183,005
49	$ 0	$ 219,960	$ 2,000	$ 207,206
50	$ 0	$ 246,355	$ 2,000	$ 234,310
51	$ 0	$ 275,917	$ 2,000	$ 264,668
52	$ 0	$ 309,028	$ 2,000	$ 298,668
53	$ 0	$ 346,111	$ 2,000	$ 336,748
54	$ 0	$ 387,644	$ 2,000	$ 379,398
55	$ 0	$ 434,161	$ 2,000	$ 427,166
56	$ 0	$ 486,261	$ 2,000	$ 480,665
57	$ 0	$ 544,612	$ 2,000	$ 540,585
58	$ 0	$ 609,966	$ 2,000	$ 607,695
59	$ 0	$ 683,162	$ 2,000	$ 682,859
60	$ 0	$ 765,141	$ 2,000	$ 767,042
61	$ 0	$ 865,958	$ 2,000	$ 861,327
62	$ 0	$ 959,793	$ 2,000	$ 966,926

Let time work for you — not against you. Start early!

Killing Time Murders Opportunity

4. Live below your means. Most of the time, we hear the advice "live within your means." Generally, that translates to "spend whatever you make." That is very poor advice!

I had the privilege of meeting a man whose name appeared on the Forbes 400, a list of the richest people in America. He started out as a high school teacher and ended up owning a very large and successful company. When asked his secret for obtaining his wealth, he responded, "By not living within my means but by living well below my means." Even when he made his first million, he and his family lived the same way they did when he was teaching school. Instead of spending his newly found wealth to "keep up with the Jones's," he saved and allowed their money to grow and compound. Living below your means is sound financial advice!

> **"Annual income twenty pounds, annual expenditure nineteen nineteen six, result – happiness. Annual income twenty pounds, annual expenditure twenty pounds ought and six, result – misery."**
> **—Charles Dickens**

5. Pay yourself first (after tithes and offerings). One of the most important steps to achieve financial independence does not involve picking the right investments. It's far more important to develop the habit of paying yourself first. Write a check to a savings or investment account before you pay your monthly bills. Increase the dollar amount each time you get a raise. To make sure you do pay yourself first, arrange to have an automatic bank draft from your checking or savings account.

When somebody gave me this advice several years ago, I struggled with it. I thought I wouldn't be able to pay all of my bills. Nevertheless, I gave it a try and increased the automatic bank drafts every time I would make more money. It worked. We were still able to pay our bills and save at the same time. It's amazing how the money was always there. I think it forced us to waste less money. We had to be sure the money was in the checking account every month, so we wouldn't end up paying overdraft charges. Paying yourself first is the disciplined way to get started on your road to financial freedom.

How much have you saved so far? Try this exercise at your earliest possible convenience. Warning: It's Depressing!

1. Number of years you have worked:	
2. Average annual income:	
3. Multiply #1 by #2:	
4. Total Accumulated Savings:	
5. Subtract #4 from #3:	
Total Dollars Spent =	

I told you it's depressing!

Here are six main reasons people fail financially:

1. Procrastination

2. Failure to Establish Goals

3. Ignorance of What Money Must Do to Accomplish Your Goals

4. Failure to Understand and Apply our Tax Laws

5. Failure to Develop a Winning Financial Attitude

6. Failure to Understand the Impact of Inflation

I'll talk more about the first five reasons people fail throughout this book. The sixth reason – inflation – can devastate you financially if you don't understand how it works against you. The following illustration shows how inflation can destroy someone's purchasing power and financial plan:

Something costing $1.00 in 1980 costs $2.46 at the end of 2006. Put another way, a retiree receiving a $1,000/month pension check in 1980 now requires $2,460/month to buy the same goods and services they purchased in 1980. That's an increase of 146%! Most people do not have a plan to increase their retirement income by 146% over a 25-30 year period of time; yet, many retirees will be retired that long before they pass away. Inflation is your enemy!

When factoring the impact of taxes and inflation on a typical safe investment, you can see in the following illustration that, quite often, you actually lose money.

What's the Real Return on CDs?

Year	CD Rate	Less Top Federal Tax Rate	Less Inflation	Real Return
1987	7.21	38.5	4.41	0.02
1988	8.18	28.0	4.42	1.41
1989	9.46	28.0	4.65	2.07
1990	8.49	28.0	6.11	0.01
1991	6.06	31.0	3.06	1.08
1992	3.82	31.0	2.90	-0.26
1993	3.34	39.6	2.75	-0.71
1994	5.05	39.6	2.67	0.37
1995	6.16	39.6	2.54	1.15
1996	5.61	39.6	3.32	0.06
1997	5.87	39.6	1.70	1.81
1998	5.58	39.6	1.61	1.73
1999	5.59	39.6	2.68	0.67
2000	6.79	39.6	3.39	0.69
2001	3.69	39.1	1.55	0.69
2002	1.81	38.6	2.38	-1.24
2003	1.23	35.0	1.88	-1.06
2004	1.75	35.0	3.94	-2.70
2005	3.79	35.0	3.04	-0.56
2006	5.33	35.0	2.04	1.40

The Toll of Inflation and Taxation on CD Return Rates

In six of the last 20 years, CDs earned a negative "real" rate of return. And in seven of the 14 positive years, CDs earned less than a 1% real rate of return.

Certificates of Deposit are FDIC insured and offer a fixed rate of return, whereas both the principal and yield of investment securities, whether stocks, bonds, or other investments, have market risk and may fluctuate with changes in market condition.

Here's another example all of us can relate to — the average cost of an automobile in 1980 was $7,530. In the year 2006, the cost more than tripled to $27,800.* Based on an assumed inflation rate of 4%, the estimated cost of a new automobile in the year 2020 will be an astounding $54,602!!

Is your lack of knowledge on how money works keeping you out of the Promised Land?

Despite The High Cost Of Living, It's Still Quite Popular

Chapter 5

Stewardship 101

Stewardship Is Not How Much You Have, It Is How You Use What You Have

Think about this. I was a quarter of a million dollars in debt. (I remember thinking I would have to be born again and again and again—to live long enough to be able to pay off all that debt.) I had a choice; I could have filed for bankruptcy, or I could have worked for the next 30-40 years just to pay off the $250,000 I owed.

I personally didn't think that filing for bankruptcy was the right thing to do. Filing for bankruptcy is legal, and, unfortunately, too many people take advantage of the "system." Just because something is legal doesn't necessarily make it morally right. (Just because prostitution is legal in Nevada, doesn't mean it's right in God's eyes!) I chose to pay the $250,000 off, so I contacted all the creditors and told them that somehow I would pay them back. We worked out repayment schedules, and, as it turned out, it only took us eight years, not several lifetimes. It's amazing how God opened the windows of heaven once we began to pay everyone back. God's stewardship principles work "big time," but He couldn't begin to bless our family until we took care of our past due financial obligations first.

In less than a decade, we were debt-free! God has blessed us more than we could ever ask or think — just like he blessed Job. Even though Job went through severe trials and tribulations, in the end, God blessed him ten-fold. Although I didn't go through what Job did, God has blessed us in the same way. He has blessed us ten thousand-fold. It is a true miracle of God. I remember asking God, "Why, Lord, did you choose us — to bless us?" (We certainly didn't deserve a second chance. Our financial ruin was my fault, not His!) That same day, He revealed the following scripture to me — "Thou has chosen the base things of this world so no flesh can glory in His presence (I Cor. 1:28,29).". Our miraculous turnaround was to bring glory to His name, not ours! Truly, God is the God of second chances. Amen!

Every disadvantage has an advantage.
—Luis Palau

II Peter 2:19 tells us, *"For a man is a slave to whatever has mastered him."* When you are in debt, you are in bondage. I know bondage firsthand; it made life so difficult. It was hard to go to church on Sunday morning to praise and worship God, when I had the bill collectors pounding on my door and calling on the phone four or five times a day, being nasty to me, my wife and our kids. It was bondage! When you are in bondage, you can't worship, pray, or witness effectively. That's not what God intended. Jesus said, *"I have come to give you life and that more abundantly."*

Stewardship is a theme throughout the Bible, yet many Christians think money is an ungodly thing. It can be used as an ungodly tool, but it also can be used as a Godly tool. I used to think that God wasn't interested in money, but that's not true. Just like salvation, stewardship principles are mentioned in the Bible, from Genesis to Revelation – just like the plan of salvation. If you look for it, you will find it.

Webster's dictionary defines stewardship as: someone who manages another's property; or a trust granted for profitable use. "Another's property" — not our own, but someone else's. "Trust granted for profitable use." I think that's interesting. The first thing that we have to realize is that what we have is from God; it's on loan from Him. Everything is God-given. John 3:27 says, "A man can receive only what is given him from heaven." I Corinthian 4:7 says, "What do you have that you did not already receive." Stewardship, simply put, is managing God's property for profitable use.

Read the parable of the talents in the book of Matthew 25:14-30, a familiar parable about the Lord going away and giving talents to three men — one received five talents, one received two talents, and one received one talent. The men with the five talents and two talents doubled the Lord's money, but the man with one talent had dug a hole and buried the money. What was the condemnation? Everything that he had was taken away from him. Think about this — people often question why the rich get richer and the poor get poorer. The rich are generally good stewards, and the poor are not. So, it's taken away from the poor and given to the rich, because they are better stewards. God can entrust them with more.

I love to read. I can generally read 25 books in any given year. I'm partial to biographies. Two of my favorites were about John D. Rockefeller and Sam Walton. John D. Rockefeller was the richest man of his day (the first billionaire in the United States). Mr. Rockefeller understood stewardship from an early age. When he was making just $25/month at his first job, he not only tithed, but he also supported the church and various missionary causes. By the time he died, some 75 years later, it was said that he had given away over one billion dollars to various ministries, colleges, hospital research projects, and conservation causes. He couldn't give it away fast enough. He was making millions daily. The Rockefeller Foundation was formed to help give it away faster and more efficiently. (God found someone He could trust with money.)

Sam Walton, the founder of the Wal-Mart stores, was also a very wealthy man — a multi-billionaire, the richest man in America. By his own admission, Mr. Walton never claimed to be religious or to have a religious experience. He did, however, understand stewardship. He stated in his autobiography that he felt a "calling" to use his wealth to help mankind, not to hoard it. His family has given away millions over the past 25 years. (Again, God found someone He could use.)

My point is that stewardship is a "law" of God. God is looking for vehicles or conduits to administer His wealth. Having trouble believing me? Look at the parable of the talents again — Matthew 25: 14-30, specifically verse 29 — *"For to everyone who has will more be given, and he will have abundance; but from him who has not, even what he has will be taken away."* That's why the rich get richer, and the poor get poorer.

A successful person is someone who has formed the habit of doing the things that unsuccessful people will not do.

Allow me to share 10 stewardship principles that changed our lives:

- **Principle #1:** Pay your bills on time. Proverbs 3:27 tells us, *"Don't withhold payment of your debts."* Romans 13:3, a familiar scripture, says, *"Owe no man anything."* We should pay our bills on time. Although that may seem fairly obvious, do we practice it? When I was going through all my financial problems, I'd be two or three months behind in our car payment, and, yet, I justified going away on vacation and spending money on myself. Was that right? Owe no man anything. How can we justify self-gratification of any kind, including going out to the movies or dinner, when we are behind on bills? If you have the money, pay your bills when they are due.

In the middle of my financial difficulties, I took our staff out to lunch for Secretary's Day. When we got back to the office, I got a call from a vendor to whom we were 90 days behind on our payment. The conversation with the vendor went something like this, "How dare you! How do you justify going out to lunch and spending the money that you have owed me for so long?" He was right. I was wrong.

If you are past due, get current as soon as possible. If you have had past credit issues and problems, here is a helpful hint regarding your credit history. It is advisable that you check your credit history every one to two years. A derogatory check mark on your credit report can ruin you. It may mean higher interest rates, inability to obtain a loan, credit card, or even to buy a house. Each individual state has its own laws pertaining to credit reporting to protect you. If you disagree with anything on your credit report, you can challenge it and, in most cases, have it removed.

Go to www.freecreditreports.com to get copies or information on how to obtain your credit reports. There are multiple credit reporting agencies. You should check them all. There are also companies that can help you clean up your credit history – for a fee, of course. They were very helpful in straightening out our very messy credit history after we paid everyone off. Check the Yellow Pages or do a search on the Internet under credit repair.

- **Principle #2:** Save money. Proverbs 21:20 says, *"A wise man saves for the future, but a foolish man spends what he gets."* This might be obvious to you, but it wasn't obvious to me. I had millions of dollars go through my hands. All I had to show for it was five dollars in our savings account, when we were forced to close the business and give up everything. Five dollars, after going through millions! What a horrible testimony that was! There is nothing ungodly about storing up for the future. It's good stewardship. Hoarding is a different story. To save for your retirement, to save for your children's college, to save to buy a home –– there is nothing wrong with that. Absolutely nothing.

If you're waiting for your favorite pyramid scheme or get-rich-quick scheme to make your dreams come true or your $20/week investment in lottery tickets to pay off soon, you're not a "wise man."

In fact, the Word says you're a fool. God said it; don't get mad at me! *"He that hasteth to be rich hath an evil eye, and considereth not that poverty shall come upon him ."* (Proverbs 28:22)

The rich save first and spend the rest; the poor spend first and save what's left, if any.

- **Principle #3:** Don't co-sign for someone else. Proverbs 17:18 says, *"It is poor judgment to countersign another's note, to become responsible for his debts."* I met with a client whose goal was to retire early. A number of years ago, he worked for a large company and was 55 years old at the time. He wanted me to evaluate his finances to see if he could retire comfortably and not have any future worries about money. After looking everything over and putting a plan together for him, he happily retired. It seemed as if he was financially set for life. I hadn't heard from him in about six or seven years. He had been getting his monthly check from his investments and was doing fine in Florida. Then, one day he called me and said, "Rich, I need a check for $65,000." I told him that wasn't part of the plan. He then informed me that he had co-signed for his son's house.

His son had been a state trooper and bought a house in New Haven, Connecticut. We all know state employees don't lose their jobs, do they? We all know that houses always go up in value, don't they? So, that being the case, why shouldn't he co-sign for the house? The answer is... things happen, such as recessions. The son lost his job, didn't have anything saved, and walked away from his financial obligation to the bank. He left the keys in the door and a note to the bank that said, "Here's your house." Who did the bank go after? Daddy. Now –– here's daddy, 62 years old, not wanting to go back to work. To make matters worse, the housing market plummeted. The house now had negative equity (worth less than what was owed). Dear old dad was stuck and had no recourse. The scripture says it is poor judgment to co-sign for someone else's debt. I agree!

Here's another quick story that may save you a bundle. Early in my church life (before my financial problems set in), a couple of young men in our church asked me if I would co-sign a bank note so they could borrow money to start a landscaping business. I thought it was the "Christian" thing to do, but, before I went ahead, I thought I would discuss it with my pastor. He opened the Bible to Proverbs 17:18. Thank God he did! I gracefully declined. It was only two to three years later that the landscaping business failed. I never asked them who was stuck with the loan, but I'm very glad it wasn't me.

Parents and grandparents — if your children need money, say no or give it to them; don't lend it to them. (I say this from experience.) Although you won't find it in scripture, lending just creates friction in the household. Saying "no" sometimes is the right thing to do. If your children don't know how to handle money, why give it to them? If you do, you're just applying a Band-Aid to a much bigger problem. Make them go for financial counseling or take a financial course before you give in.

Neither a borrower nor a lender be.
—William Shakespeare

- **Principle #4:** Do not go into debt. No one willingly wants to get into debt. Proverbs 22:7 says, *"Just as the rich rule over the poor, so the borrower is servant to the lender."* I remember finally starting to "see the light at the end of the tunnel" financially. I said to my wife, "Let's give the kids a great Christmas." We felt guilty as parents that we weren't able to do much for them for the last four or five years. We went "all out" that Christmas, and the kids ended up playing with the empty boxes and the bows. Why do we go into debt just to have a great Christmas, to drive a nicer car than our friends, to live in a bigger house than our relatives, or to go on better vacations than our co-worker? Why? It doesn't have to be that way! If you can't afford it to begin with, why put it on a credit card and get further into debt by paying an additional 10% to 20% interest and making payments for years? It's going to be broken by the time you pay it off anyway. I was a "slave" to debt when the sheriff showed up at the door on a regular basis, trying to repossess everything we had. You don't want to be a "slave"; don't get into debt. It's not worth it. The pressure can kill you.

"And he said onto them, take heed, and beware of covetousness: For a man's life consisteth not in the abundance of the things which he possesseth." (Luke 12:15)

There is a big difference between need and greed.
—Rev. Todd Foster

If you are "in over your head", there is help. The Consumer Credit Counseling Service (CCCS) helps individuals with putting a plan together to pay off your creditors. In many cases, they can freeze your accounts, so no additional interest is charged if you make the agreed upon payment. CCCS is a not-for-profit organization and can be reached at 800-388-2227.

"Failure to prepare is preparing to fail."
—John Wooden

- **Principle #5:** Plan properly. Proverbs 24:3-4 tells us "Any Enterprise built on wise planning becomes strong through common sense and profits wonderfully by keeping abreast of the facts." Any enterprise, whether it is your household, your business, your job, your school or church, should be built by wise planning, using common sense, and by keeping abreast of the facts. In my opinion, that means using a budget in your home. If you have a business, then you should have a business plan. There's nothing wrong with doing these kinds of things. It's just one of the components of being a good steward. Luke 14:28-30 says "For which of you, desiring to build a tower, does not first sit down and count the cost, whether he has enough to complete it? Otherwise, when he has laid a foundation, and is not able to finish, all who see it begin to mock him, saying, 'This man began to build, and was not able to finish.'"

Proper planning is critical to success. Ever wonder why most small businesses stay small? They think small, plan small, do things on a small scale. If you want your business to become a larger business, then think, plan and execute on a bigger scale. The Everett Financial Group, Inc. became one of the country's largest independent financial planning firms by learning what the "big guys" did. Success doesn't just happen. You have to plan properly at each level to be able to move to the next level.

As Long as You're Going to Think Anyway, You Might As Well Think Big!
—Donald Trump

I must admit I get a kick out of frequently telling the following story (and I don't mean to pick on any kind of trade, individual, or group). I am the most unhandy person on this planet. I need help to do anything around the house. My wife says, "Call somebody. Don't let Richard fix it."

So, I'll call an electrician, carpenter, plumber, or painter when something needs to be repaired. They tell you they're going to be at your house at 8 o'clock in the morning, and they never even show up. That's never happened to you? It happens all the time. It's ridiculous! Why are they in business? They need the work, right? I guess not.

I get on my "soap box" all the time about this. If you're goi
own your business, then let your "nay" be nay and your "yea" be yea. In
other words, keep your word, and plan accordingly. If you say you'll be
somewhere, then be there —— and on time. It perplexes me how these
tradesmen spend thousands of dollars to advertise their businesses and
then they don't ever show up. If you're a man or woman who keeps your
word, how many referrals will you get from satisfied and happy customers?
You won't have to spend all that money on advertising.

The scripture says you need to plan properly. Yes, you have heard it
a hundred times — "People don't plan to fail, they simply fail to plan."
Now you have heard it 101 times, so plan already! Stop talking about it;
do it! As Tom Landry, the legendary coach of the Dallas Cowboys, said,
"The quality of a man's life is in direct proportion to his commitment to
excellence." Excellence doesn't just happen. Planning properly will help
you achieve excellence.

Here is Jesus' explanation of stewardship: *"He who is faithful in what is
least is faithful also in much; and he who is unjust in what is least is unjust also
in much. Therefore, if you have not been faithful in the unrighteous mammon,
who will commit to your trust the true riches?"* (Luke 16:10-11)

I would rather try something and fail than try nothing and succeed.
—Rev. Charles Stanley

Successful people move on their own initiative and they know where they are going before they start.

- Principle #6: Don't cheat. Proverbs 20:10 says, *"The Lord despises
  every kind of cheating."* What kind of cheating? Every kind of cheating.
  When I counsel people, the first thing we have to determine in the
  counseling session is — "Are you cheating?" Sometimes they look at
  me cross-eyed or with glazed eyes, saying, "Are we cheating? What
  do you mean?" Are you cheating the Lord on your tithes? Are you
  cheating your employer by showing up late or taking things that
  don't belong to you? If you're self-employed, are you cheating the
  IRS? It's so easy as a self-employed individual to write yourself a
  check, say it's for business purposes, and stick it in your pocket.

"For unless you are honest in small matters, you won't be in honest with greater responsibilities. And if you are untrustworthy about worldly wealth, who will trust you with the true riches of heaven? And if you are not faithful with other people's money, why should you be entrusted with money of your own?" (Luke 16:10-12)

Remember, God sees everything. And what does the scripture say? If you can't be entrusted with the least, how do you expect to be entrusted more? In other words, if a person can't be a good steward with $100 or cheats the IRS out of taxes, how can God possibly bless that person? The Lord despises every kind of cheat in — not some. I am not a fan of the IRS, and I don't like writing out those checks either, but you need to do what is right all the time — no matter what the cost! In Matthew 22:21, the Pharisees asked the question, *"Is it lawful to pay taxes to Caesar?"* Jesus responded with, *"Render to Caesar the things that are Caesar's."*

"The best chance you have of making a big success in this world is to decide from square one that you are going to do it ethically."
"What you're going to find is not necessarily that, if you are ethical, you will succeed, but the probability that you will is significantly greater than if you are not."
—Alan Greenspan

Food for thought –– Is buying lotto tickets or going to the casino cheating? Whose money is it anyway — God's or yours? One might say, "But if I win the lotto, I can bless my church, give to missionaries, contribute to the building fund, etc." No, you won't! If you're not faithful with what you have now, you won't be faithful if you win the lotto. Besides, what makes you think God will allow you to win anyway? Everyone is after the get-rich-quick scheme. Not many want to work for it. According to USA Today, your odds of winning a million dollars in the lotto are 12,000,000 to 1, and your odds of winning the slots in a casino are 6,000,000 to 1. One dollar a day (the cost of a lotto ticket), invested in a good mutual fund over 40 years, can potentially grow to well over a million dollars!

The problem with instant gratification is that it takes too long.

- **Principle #7:** Work hard. Proverbs 10:4 tells us to work hard. *"Lazy men are soon poor while hard workers get rich."* Ephesians 5:16 also says, *"Make the most of your time."* My goal and your goal should never be to get rich. We need to keep our priorities right. About five years ago, a pastor had sent me two couples for counseling. They came from the same church, with the same problems. They were in debt "up to their eyeballs." I started the sessions with my usual question –– Are you cheating? I discovered neither couple was tithing, nor did they have budgets. I sent both couples away with the same challenge. Put God first in the area of finances, and He will bless you and help you get out of debt. The first couple came back the next week and decided to start tithing. I put a plan and a budget together for them, and they were out of debt within one year. The other couple has yet to come back. That was over 10 years ago, and they are still in debt. The husband bounces back and forth from job to job, getting nowhere. The first couple enjoys a debt-free, bondage-free life. They worked hard and were willing to "pay the price." The second couple was lazy, and they're paying the price for their laziness — being debt-ridden and miserable. Killing time murders opportunities!

"A little sleep, a little slumber, a little folding of the hands to rest, and poverty will come on you like a bandit and scarcity like an armed man (Proverbs 24:33-34)."

"Six days shalt thou labor, and do all thy work (Exodus 20:9)."

"In all labor there is profit (Proverbs 15:23)."

"Whatsoever thy hand findeth to do, do it with thy might; For there is no work, nor device, nor knowledge, nor wisdom, in the grave, wither thou goest (Ecclesiastes 9:10)."

"Be strong — and work; For I am with you, says the Lord (Haggai 2:4)."

The Only Difference Between Success and Failure is Luck — Just Ask Any Failure

- **Principle #8:** Strive to have a good reputation. Proverbs 22:1 says, *"If you must choose, take a good name rather than great riches. For to be held in loving esteem is better than silver or gold."* I love telling the following story of a gentleman named Bruce, who was a member of a church I attended a number of years ago. He got up on a Sunday night church service and gave the following testimony. "I want to thank God I lost my job this week." (And he wasn't trying to be a wise guy.) He continued, "I know when God closes one door, He's going to open another door, a better door." Now, here's a man with two children and one on the way, sincerely thanking God that he lost his job. Bruce was a foreman for a good-sized construction company. When we hit a recession, the company was forced to close its doors. People in the church who needed a porch, an addition, a deck, etc. started hiring him. Bruce always went the extra mile, did great work, and showed up on time! The rest is history. He has such a good reputation that he has yet to spend a dime on advertising. He has jobs lined up for over a year, because people want Bruce to do the work. Are customers or clients not referring you? Are you not getting the raises or promotions you think you deserve? What are people saying about you? What kind of reputation do you have?

"I therefore, the prisoner of the Lord, beseech you that ye walk worthy of the vocation wherewith ye are called (Ephesians 4:1)."

"Good Enough Never Is"
—Debbie Fields
Founder, Mrs. Fields Cookies

- **Principle #9:** Stand up under pressure. Proverbs 24:10 tells us, *"You are a poor specimen if you can't stand the pressures of adversity."* Did you know that Christians will have adversities? God actually allows us to go through them. Adversities make us better people. When I was broke, I remember praying, "Lord, I want to get close to you, closer than I've ever been before." Every time I would pray, my financial problems would get worse. The next week I would say, "Lord, I want to get closer to you," and things would get worse. I finally realized that He was answering my prayers. As we went through all the problems, and things worsened, we would draw closer to Him. "You are a poor specimen if you cannot stand the pressure." There is no reason to give up. God will see you through. I'm a living testimony to God's goodness. Looking back over the past 20 years, going through a financial collapse was the best thing that ever happened to me. God has taught me so much over the years. I know now what good stewardship is. I know how to handle money and to be found faithful with it. God has now entrusted me with more wealth than I could have ever dreamed. If I hadn't gone through financial ruin, I wouldn't be where I am today. Thank you, Lord!

Here's something very valuable I learned over the years from counseling couples. Contrary to popular belief, the lack of finances is not the number one cause of marital strife and/or divorce. Many times, that's the excuse or reason given, but the reality is, it's the lack of the three "C's" – communication, consecration, and commitment. Couples rarely talk about money. They usually fight instead. They don't turn their finances over to the Lord (consecration) and His principles. There is no commitment to staying out of debt, tithing and being good stewards of God's money. They also lack a commitment to each other. "Until death do us part" is pretty much self-explanatory.

Success Is Never Painless

- **Principle #10:** Make provisions for difficult times. All of us are going to have difficult times. Count on it! Proverbs 22:3 says, "It is a prudent man who foresees the difficulties ahead and prepares for them. The simpleton goes blindly on and suffers the consequences."

Here's another quick story... We have friends who live in Massachusetts. A number of years ago, in the midst of an economic boom, we were having pizza together. The man was in business also. We were discussing how the economy could not continue to grow as it had for the past several years. It was too good. Real estate prices were going crazy, and wages were going up at outrageous rates. We looked at each other and said, "We're going to hit a recession. The good times can't continue forever." We both decided to reduce our debt down as much as possible. I thought, if we hit a recession, I'm not going to have the same problems I had before. He's in the computer industry and said, "If I ever lose my job, I'm going to lose my house. I'm going to go back and work on becoming debt-free." Sure enough, 18 months later, we went into one of the worst recessions the state of Connecticut had ever seen. We made provisions for the difficult times. We saw the difficulties ahead and planned accordingly.

Here's an example of the "flip side of that coin"–– Many realtors went out of business in the early 90s because they didn't see the difficulties ahead. If you go back to the economic boom, realtors were making money "hand over fist" because properties were selling "like hot cakes." What did they do with the money? Most spent it. Many had their Mercedes and vacation homes repossessed when the bad times came. They didn't see the difficulties ahead; wages couldn't keep pace with the escalating prices for homes. Sooner or later, the bottom had to fall out. A prudent man foresees the difficulties ahead and prepares, and the simpleton goes on blindly and suffers the consequences. Those who ignore their past mistakes are doomed to repeat them! Remember – Noah built an ark before it started to rain!

If you're not winning, perhaps you don't know the rules or how the gamed is played.

Let me give you two examples of the benefits of good stewardship:

Example #1: Back in 1986 or so, I had begun to experience substantial growth in my financial planning practice. We needed a computer desperately. Desktop computers were not nearly as inexpensive as they are today, and I didn't want to spend a lot of money on a computer that would be outdated in two to three years. So, I prayed and asked the Lord to provide us with a low cost machine. I didn't want to waste God's money. I simply said, "If you want us to have a computer, you'll need to supply it for us." Remember — I had just gone through a business failure, and I didn't want to blow the money. Three or four weeks later, a gentleman from the office across the hall came in to see me. He had just purchased a new state-of-the-art computer and wanted to know if I knew of anyone interested in purchasing his year old model. He only wanted $500, but it needed some repairs first to fix a couple of minor problems. I gladly accepted. While it was in the repair shop being fixed, it was stolen! The repair shop replaced my year old computer with a brand new computer at a cost to me of $500! Thank God!

Example #2: Around the same time, I needed a receptionist. Again, I didn't want to spend the money or time by placing an ad in the paper or to hire an employment agency. I again prayed and asked the Lord to provide me with the right person at the right time. About a month later, I received a call from a colleague, who asked me if I knew anyone who needed to hire a receptionist. The colleague's office was closing, and the receptionist was looking for a job. Mary, our excellent receptionist, worked with us until she retired.

Yes, God does answer prayers, and He honors our attempts to be good stewards!

Here is what Jesus has to say about stewardship: *"And the Lord said, who then is that faithful steward, the wise man whom his master will set over those in his household service, to supply them their allowance of food at the appointed time? Blessed – happy, and to be envied. Is that servant whom his master finds so doing when he arrives. Truly, I tell you, he will set him in charge over all his possessions."* (Luke 12:42-44)

The Bible's Best Stewardship Illustration

One of the greatest stories in the Bible about stewardship is found in Genesis 41. Joseph is taken out of prison to interpret the Pharaoh's dream. Seven years of plenty, followed by seven years of famine was the interpretation. Joseph had a plan to take 20% of all the harvest and store it up so that they could have food in the time of need. What a great story of stewardship! Read it; it's powerful!

Genesis 41:1-57

When two full years had passed, Pharaoh had a dream: He was standing by the Nile, when out of the river there came up seven cows, sleek and fat, and they grazed among the reeds. After them, seven other cows, ugly and gaunt, came up out of the Nile and stood beside those on the riverbank. And the cows that were ugly and gaunt ate up the seven sleek, fat cows. Then Pharaoh woke up. He fell asleep again and had a second dream: Seven heads of grain, healthy and good, were growing on a single stalk. After them, seven other heads of grain sprouted—thin and scorched by the east wind. The thin heads of grain swallowed up the seven healthy, full heads. Then Pharaoh woke up; it had been a dream. In the morning his mind was troubled, so he sent for all the magicians and wise men of Egypt. Pharaoh told them his dreams, but no one could interpret them for him.

Then the chief cupbearer said to Pharaoh, "Today I am reminded of my shortcomings. Pharaoh was once angry with his servants, and he imprisoned me and the chief baker in the house of the captain of the guard. Each of us had a dream the same night, and each dream had a meaning of its own. Now a young Hebrew was there with us, a servant of the captain of the guard. We told him our dreams, and he interpreted them for us, giving each man the interpretation of his dream. And things turned out exactly as he interpreted them to us: I was restored to my position, and the other man was hanged."

So Pharaoh sent for Joseph, and he was quickly brought from the dungeon. When he had shaved and changed his clothes, he came before Pharaoh. Pharaoh said to Joseph, "I had a dream, and no one can interpret it. But I have heard it said of you that when you hear a dream you can interpret it." "I cannot do it," Joseph replied to Pharaoh, "but God will give Pharaoh the answer he desires."

Then Pharaoh said to Joseph, "In my dream I was standing on the bank of the Nile, when out of the river there came up seven cows, fat and sleek, and they grazed among the reeds. After them, seven other cows came up—scrawny and very ugly and lean. I had never seen such ugly cows in all the land of Egypt. The lean, ugly cows ate up the seven fat cows that came up first. But even after they ate them, no one could tell that they had done so; they looked just as ugly as before. Then I woke up.

"In my dreams I also saw seven heads of grain, full and good, growing on a single stalk. After them, seven other heads sprouted—withered and thin and scorched by the east wind. The thin heads of grain swallowed up the seven good heads. I told this to the magicians, but none could explain it to me."

Then Joseph said to Pharaoh, "The dreams of Pharaoh are one and the same. God has revealed to Pharaoh what he is about to do. The seven good cows are seven years, and the seven good heads of grain are seven years; it is one and the same dream. The seven lean, ugly cows that came up afterward are seven years, and so are the seven worthless heads of grain scorched by the east wind: They are seven years of famine.

"It is just as I said to Pharaoh: God has shown Pharaoh what he is about to do. Seven years of great abundance are coming throughout the land of Egypt, but seven years of famine will follow them. Then all the abundance in Egypt will be forgotten, and the famine will ravage the land. The abundance in the land will not be remembered, because the famine that follows it will be so severe. The reason the dream was given to Pharaoh in two forms is that the matter has been firmly decided by God, and God will do it soon.

"And now let Pharaoh look for a discerning and wise man and put him in charge of the land of Egypt. Let Pharaoh appoint commissioners over the land to take a fifth of the harvest of Egypt during the seven years of abundance. They should collect all the food of these good years that are coming and store up the grain under the authority of Pharaoh, to be kept in the cities for food. This food should be held in reserve for the country, to be used during the seven years of famine that will come upon Egypt, so that the country may not be ruined by the famine."

The plan seemed good to Pharaoh and to all his officials. So Pharaoh asked them, "Can we find anyone like this man, one in whom is the spirit of God?" Then Pharaoh said to Joseph, "Since God has made all this known to you, there is no one so discerning and wise as you. You shall be in charge of my palace, and all my people are to submit to your orders. Only with respect to the throne will I be greater than you."

So Pharaoh said to Joseph, "I hereby put you in charge of the whole land of Egypt." Then Pharaoh took his signet ring from his finger and put it on Joseph's finger. He dressed him in robes of fine linen and put a gold chain around his neck. He had him ride in a chariot as his second-in-command, and men shouted before him, "Make way!" Thus he put him in charge of the whole land of Egypt. Then Pharaoh said to Joseph, "I am Pharaoh, but without your word no one will lift hand or foot in all Egypt."

Pharaoh gave Joseph the name Zaphenath-Paneah and gave him Asenath daughter of Potiphera, priest of On, to be his wife. And Joseph went throughout the land of Egypt. Joseph was thirty years old when he entered the service of Pharaoh king of Egypt. And Joseph went out from Pharaoh's presence and traveled throughout Egypt.

During the seven years of abundance the land produced plentifully. Joseph collected all the food produced in those seven years of abundance in Egypt and stored it in the cities. In each city he put the food grown in the fields surrounding it. Joseph stored up huge quantities of grain, like the sand of the sea; it was so much that he stopped keeping records because it was beyond measure.

Before the years of famine came, two sons were born to Joseph by Asenath daughter of Potiphera, priest of On. Joseph named his firstborn Manasseh and said, "It is because God has made me forget all my trouble and all my father's household." The second son he named Ephraim and said, "It is because God has made me fruitful in the land of my suffering."

The seven years of abundance in Egypt came to an end, and the seven years of famine began, just as Joseph had said. There was famine in all the other lands, but in the whole land of Egypt there was food. When all Egypt began to feel the famine, the people cried to Pharaoh for food. Then Pharaoh told all the Egyptians, "Go to Joseph and do what he tells you." When the famine had spread over the whole country, Joseph opened the storehouses and sold grain to the Egyptians, for the famine was severe throughout Egypt. And all the countries came to Egypt to buy grain from Joseph, because the famine was severe in all the world.

—New International Version

Maybe saving or investing 20% of our income, instead of spending 100%, is something God wants us to do. Listen carefully, and He will direct you.

Again, I strongly urge you to read the parable of the talents, found in Matthew 25:14-30. The story clearly illustrates what God expects of us as stewards. Every time I read it, I learn something new!

"Moreover, it is required of stewards that one be found trustworthy." (I Cor. 4:2)

Chapter 6

Investing 101

As a registered financial consultant and a registered securities representative for over 20 years, I feel I am qualified to give sound investment advice. At the time this book was written, I managed nearly $150 million for over 1,000 clients.

I strongly believe it is perfectly acceptable for a Christian to invest in the stock market. Notice I said, "invest," not speculate or gamble. There is a huge difference. I also believe there is a big difference between saving and investing. We should put our money in a bank or credit union to save. We should put our money in stocks, bonds, and mutual funds to invest. A good biblical example of the difference between saving and investing can be found in the parable of the talents in Matthew Chapter

25. The master gave (entrusted) talents (money) to three of his servants and went on his journey. The servant that received five talents doubled the master's money by the time the lord returned, as did the servant given the two talents. (See The Rule of 72 at the end of this chapter.)

Assuming 6% bank rates [money changers], it would have taken 12 years to double. I don't believe they put the money there. I believe they invested it in the Mt. Zion Mutual Fund or the stock market equivalent of the day. "Well done my good and faithful servant" was the praise from their master. The third servant, who was given the one talent, returned the single talent to his master, with no gain or interest. His master replied, "You wicked, lazy servant." "The least you should have done was to deposit my money with the bankers so that when I returned I would have received it back with interest. An important point in the parable was when the master said, "The least you should have done was to deposit my money with the bankers." If putting money in the bank was the least he should have done, then I believe investing elsewhere was an option he should have used, as the other two servants must have done.

I admired the late Larry Burkett. He gave sound budgeting advice to Christians for years. His advice helped get our family out of debt and to be good stewards, but I do strongly advise staying away from his investment advice. If you took Larry's advice on investing 20-25 years ago, for the most part, you would be no better off today and, in some cases, worse off after inflation and taxes are factored in. Most of Larry's economic predictions have turned out to be dead wrong. Generally, Mr. Burkett has suggested that Christians invest in precious metals, namely gold and silver (disastrous advice), real estate, and treasury bonds or bank instruments. If, on the other hand, you had ignored his advice and invested $100,000 (25 years ago) into an S&P 500 Index fund, your money would have grown to $1,068,390, a cumulative gain of 968.39%. The same money invested in a C.D. would have grown to $588,941, a 488.94% cumulative gain. Which would you rather have? Remember, there is a big difference between saving and investing.

Read the following quotes found in the June, 2000 issue of Christianity Today:

"The predicted 'economic earthquake' (Burkett's book published in 1994) never occurred, however. In fact, the exact opposite happened – the United

States experienced a major upturn in which the stock market climbed to never-imagined heights.

"Gary Moore, who considers himself a former friend of Burkett's and now a staunch critic, thinks Burkett's main problem is a pessimistic world view. 'A lot of doom and gloomers come and go on Wall Street', Moore adds. 'But I can't remember one being as deeply pessimistic and wrong as Larry.'"

"I don't pretend to be a prophet."
—Larry Burkett

Mr. Burkett's reasoning for playing it safe with our money is the coming of a worldwide economic collapse. I do agree with Larry on this point. It is very possible a worldwide depression will be "the event" that brings the anti-Christ onto the scene. He will claim to be our "savior" and promise to get us out of the mess. When we, as a nation, are broke and desperate, we will put our faith, hope, and trust in almost anyone. This is only my opinion. I am not a theologian. However, if Larry and I are both correct, will it make any difference where our money was invested if we do go into a global depression? Food, clothing, and shelter would be the most precious resources, not gold, silver, C.D.s, treasury bonds, or stocks. In other words, a total economic catastrophe would render all investments worthless. So, why not do the best we can with what we have been entrusted with for as long as we can. Here's the bottom line — the Lord said, "Occupy till I come." I am going to do just that. Unfortunately, money doesn't come with an instruction manual; however, the rest of this chapter will help you get started on the road to investing properly.

Investment Tips for Beginners

"Buy some good stock. Hold it till it goes up — and then sell it. If it doesn't go up – don't buy it."
—Will Rogers

Investing for the first time can be scary, intimidating, and downright nerve-racking. No one wants to lose all of their hard-earned money to a bad investment — and yet, novice or first-time investors have been known to do strange and foolish things. I have met people who have never invested before and suddenly buy shares in a start-up company because they heard a "hot tip" down at the barbershop, or they buy stock they know nothing or little about because Uncle Harry was talking about it at the latest social gathering.

It's amazing to see the kind of research that goes into purchasing a new television or refrigerator; yet, we blindly throw our money into a stock with little or no research! I have encountered several individuals who have lent to or invest with a family member or close friend to open a new restaurant, retail store, or manufacturing operation — with virtually no research. Granted, some of these opportunities occasionally work out, but most do not. Unfortunately, many first-time investors lose everything and never attempt to invest again — too bad!

Investing, speculating or gambling?

There is an immense difference between investing, speculating, and gambling. The scenarios previously mentioned are speculating and gambling, not investing. Investing can be both rewarding and exciting, if done properly. Think about this — the Dow Jones Industrial Average (DJIA), an index* to measure how well or poorly the stock market has done, was at 40 in 1929 (just after the stock market crash that led into the Great Depression). At the end of 2006, the DJIA closed at 12,463. Doing some quick math, that's over a 30,000% increase! More importantly, the average annual compounded rate of return for the Dow since 1900 is just shy of 10%—not bad! (*It is not possible to invest directly in an index, and past performance may not be indicative of future returns.)

Having given you two astounding statistics, I ask the question—How could anyone have lost money in the stock market? The answer is that most people buy at the wrong time, sell at the wrong time, or don't buy the right investments.

People tend to buy what is "hot". According to the 8/28/97 Wall Street Journal, the top performing mutual fund for the previous 12 months was a Russia Fund. Thousands upon thousands of investors poured their hard-earned money into this fund that had been up an incredible 150%. Want to guess what the worst performing mutual fund was 12 months later? You guessed it! The same Russia Fund was down over 85%! Buying high and selling low is a great way to go broke!

Investing 101

Looking back to 1987 (the second stock market crash of the past century), the Dow has gained more than 400%! That's correct — theoretically, you would have doubled your money twice in less than 20 years. In order to take advantage of the incredible growth of the stock market, you should follow what I call The Six Key Principles of Investing:

Principle #1: Buy Quality

Stocks generally go up when company profits go up. There is a strong correlation between what the market does and what companies earn. Warren Buffet, chairman of Berkshire Hathaway and perhaps the most outstanding investor of our time, has made an absolute "killing" in the stock market by purchasing large blocks of well-known, well-managed industry leaders such as Coca-Cola, Gillette, Geico, and American Express.

Principle #2: Diversify

We have all heard the phrase numerous times — "Don't put all of your eggs in one basket." This philosophy is definitely true when it comes to investing. A diversified portfolio can reduce risk by dividing investment dollars among a variety of investments, such as stocks, bonds, money market funds, and real estate. The following illustration shows how diversification can help maximize growth potential while minimizing risk over time:

**Investment Results for Investor A and Investor B
Over a 20 Year Period of Time***

Investor A		Investor B	
$ 20,000 at 12% return =	$ 192,926	$ 100,000 at 5% return =	$ 265,330
$ 20,000 at 10% return =	$ 134,550		
$ 20,00 at 5% return =	$ 53,066		
$ 20,000 at break even =	$ 20,000		
$ 20,000 at total loss =	$ 0		
	$ 492,630		

$492,630
- $265,330
= $227,330 more, by diversifying instead of playing it safe.

Even if some of the investments don't do well, you still can do well with a diversified portfolio. As you can see, playing it safe can potentially cost you a bundle!

"Give a portion to seven, and also to eight, for thou knowest not what evil shall be upon the earth." (Ecclesiastes 11:2)

*Example for Illustrative Purposes Only. The numbers are hypothetical and not intended to reflect actual investment returns for any product or security.

The following are a few simple illustrations to help explain the benefits of diversification:

1. The Window Illustration

U.S. Stocks	Foreign Stocks	CD's
Real Estate		Bonds
Treasury Bonds	Money Markets	Gold

"Diversified"

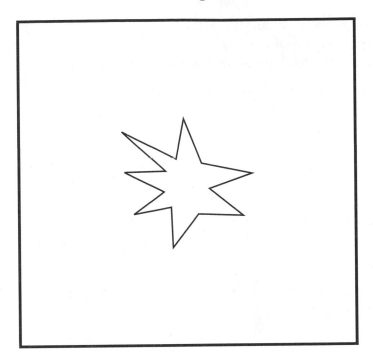

"Non-Diversified"

As you can see, the window on the left (a diversified portfolio) needs only one section/pane to be repaired after being shattered in one area. The window on the right (a non-diversified portfolio) needs to be replaced entirely, because it doesn't have separate sections/panes.

Why a Balanced Portfolio?

According to a study by SEI Corp., (the world's largest pension consulting firm):

• 93% of a portfolio's performance is determined by asset allocation.

• 7% of a portfolio's performance is determined by specific investing and market timing.

Myth: A greater return is possible only if there is a correspondingly greater risk.

Whatever Happened to the Promised Land?

Fact: Bailard, Biehl & Kaiser recently analyzed the 20-year performance history of a number of investment portfolios. They concluded that a balanced portfolio produced comparable yields with significantly less risk.

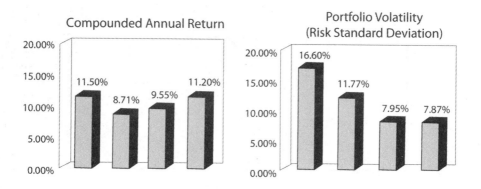

The moral of the story? You can potentially get the same investment return from a diversified portfolio (11.20%) as you can in a portfolio invested 100% in stocks (11.50%), but you can do so with half the risk, 7.87% standard deviation (risk) versus 16.60% (100% in stocks).

As you can see from the following illustration, asset classes move in and out of favor. Since no one knows which asset classes will do well next year, three years, or five years from now, it makes sense to stay diversified.

Five-year snapshot of historical allocation:

Jun 02	Sep 02	Dec 02	Mar 03	Jun 03	Sep 03	Dec 03	Mar 04	Jun 04	Sep 04
62.9%	59.9%	60.2%	52.1%	42.9%	25.7%	26.0%	35.7%	32.3%	37.9%
10.9%	11.9%	14.6%	13.6%	23.6%	20.6%	25.3%	30.8%	29.2%	29.5%
10.0%	9.3%	7.1%	11.2%	10.6%	17.9%	19.1%	11.0%	9.8%	9.7%
6.8%	6.8%	6.8%	9.7%	9.7%	11.1%	11.5%	9.0%	9.7%	8.7%
6.0%	6.6%	5.8%	8.1%	6.1%	9.0%	9.6%	6.0%	9.4%	5.1%
2.9%	5.2%	4.6%	2.7%	4.0%	8.4%	6.5%	2.8%	4.9%	4.6%
0.5%	0.4%	0.9%	1.8%	2.2%	5.1%	1.9%	2.6%	2.5%	2.9%
0.0%	0.0%	0.0%	0.8%	0.8%	2.3%	0.1%	2.0%	2.2%	2.6%

U.S. Equities			U.S. Gov/Mortgage Backed			Foreign Equities		USD Corporate Bonds	

*Holdings and composition of holdings are subject to change. *International investing involves additional risks, including currency fluctuations, political or economic conditions affecting the foreign country, and differences in accounting standards and foreign regulations. *Investing in small-cap stocks may carry more risk than investing in stocks of larger, more well-established companies.

Whatever Happened to the Promised Land?

Dec 04	Mar 05	June 05	Sep 05	Dec 05	Mar 06	Jun 06	Sep 06	Dec 06	Mar 07	Jun 07
39.8%	35.7%	38.7%	37.7%	40.9%	41.2%	31.6%	36.4%	29.6%	44.9%	53.0%
30.2%	32.0%	32.7%	35.9%	40.1%	40.2%	25.8%	22.1%	24.6%	29.6%	26.2%
7.2%	9.4%	6.5%	7.6%	4.6%	5.4%	21.0%	12.7%	18.7%	9.0%	10.8%
6.5%	6.4%	5.9%	6.2%	4.6%	4.2%	7.1%	7.9%	8.0%	4.9%	3.2%
5.3%	5.4%	5.4%	5.4%	3.4%	3.6%	5.7%	6.5%	6.5%	4.2%	2.5%
5.2%	4.5%	4.1%	3.3%	2.8%	3.4%	3.7%	6.3%	5.3%	4.1%	2.5%
3.1%	4.4%	3.5%	2.9%	2.2%	1.5%	2.6%	4.9%	3.9%	3.3%	1.9%
2.8%	2.2%	3.2%	0.9%	1.4%	0.7%	2.5%	3.2%	3.7%	0.0%	0.0%

Foreign Currency Bonds | **Gold Bulletin** | **Gold Equities** | **Convertibles** | **Cash**

*Investing in high-income securities may carry a greater risk of nonpayment of interest or principle than higher-rated bonds. *Fixed income securities are subject to interest rate risk and, as such, the net asset value of the Fund may fall as interest rates rise. *As with any mutual fund, the value of the Fund's shares will change, and you could lose money on your investment. These and other risks are more fully described in the Fund's prospectus.

Source: Ivy Funds Distributor, Inc. TMF5149 (7/07)

2. The Pencil Illustration

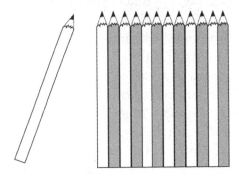

Grab a pencil and break it using both hands. That task is fairly easy. Now, take nine smaller pencils, place them together and attempt to break them in the same manner. It's virtually impossible. Imagine those pencils are your investments. If all your investments had been concentrated in that one pencil, you would have been devastated when the pencil broke. However, by spreading your assets among many investments (pencils), you have a "stronger" position that protects you if something bad happens.

Allow me to share a couple of true stories. I couldn't make these up if I wanted to!

When I started my investment career back in 1984, my manager told me about a friend of his, a pilot for Braniff Airlines. The pilot had 100% of his 401(k) in Braniff Airlines stock. As you may know, Braniff didn't go bankrupt once – but twice! Not only did the pilot lose his job but his entire retirement savings. My manager simply said, "Son, the lesson is to make sure your clients don't put all of their eggs in one basket." Sound advice that, unfortunately, far too many people ignore.

A few years into my career, a potential client, who worked for Union Carbide, came to see me. During our first meeting, he disclosed that his entire 401(k) was in Union Carbide stock. I went on to share the Braniff Airlines story, to which he responded, "Yea, but this is Union Carbide, not Braniff Airlines. Union Carbide won't go out of business." Sure enough, he was right – Union Carbide didn't go out of business. Instead of going bankrupt, the company's facility in Bhopal, India killed over 300 people. If my memory serves me correctly, his 401(k) declined by over 50% within just a few short weeks of the disaster.

Whatever Happened to the Promised Land?

Not too long after my Union Carbide employee encounter, a middle-aged gentleman came to my office, who was employed by Exxon. He had $400,000 in a 401(k) – all in Exxon stock. My first suggestion to him was to diversify his 401(k) into some of the other options within his retirement plan. After telling him my Braniff Airlines and Union Carbide stories, he reluctantly moved 25% of his Exxon stock into some of the additional investment options. He reminded me that the Exxon Corporation was at the top of the Fortune 500 list and nothing could possibly happen, but, nevertheless, the diversification made sense. Sure enough, within six months of our meeting, a drunken sea captain drives his Exxon oil tanker where he shouldn't have to create the Valdez oil spill. If I'm not mistaken, Exxon stock declined by at least half. My new client's 401(k) was no longer worth $400,000. If he had he not heeded my advice, it could have been worse.

Not too long after Valdez, a gentleman who attended one of my seminars came to see me. He was an IBM employee. In fact, he was one of the original employees. He was 64 ½ years old and was getting ready to retire in six months. How does he have his 401(k) invested? You guessed it – all $550,000 in IBM stock. I went on to tell him my Braniff, Union Carbide, and Exxon stories, to which he replied, "Yes, but this is IBM – nothing like that could ever happen to IBM." Wrong! The year was 1990. Any idea what happened to IBM that year? Fifty thousand people were laid off, the new CEO was asked to leave, and the company had lost millions upon millions of dollars. My seminar attendee called me back after turning 65, literally crying, wanting to know if there was anything I could do. IBM stock declined nearly $100 per share in that short period of time. His 401(k) was now worth less than $200,000. (I guess you can now call it a 201k.) He did not retire but was forced to continue to work several more years until the stock rebounded. What a shame, because it didn't have to happen!

A few years ago, a couple came to see me. The husband had 100% of his 401(k) in Aetna stock worth $320,000. He was getting ready to retire soon. I went on to tell him my Braniff, Union Carbide, Exxon, and IBM stories. His wife looked at him and said, "If you don't sell your Aetna stock tomorrow, I'll shoot you. He (referring to me) is the kiss of death."

The gentleman sold 100% of his Aetna stock the next day. The following week, Aetna announced disappointing earnings. The stock declined $25 per share in a day and $15 per share the following day.

Finally... a happy ending... someone who took the advice and properly diversified!

Oh yes... and then there was Enron!

Remember the three "D's" of investing: Diversify, Diversify, Diversify!

Principle #3: Buy Systematically

Simply put, systematic investing means making regular investments at set intervals over time. This disciplined approach allows you to focus on long-term financial goals and not on the short-term ups and downs of the market. When you invest systematically, you buy more shares when prices are low (think of them as being on sale) and fewer shares when prices increase. This concept is also called dollar cost averaging*. If you invested just $100/month for 30 years in one of the mutual funds that has actually been around that long, your investment has grown to over $500,000 — a 12.5% average annual return. Dollar cost averaging, to say the least, can be very effective!

If you make regular payments to your company-sponsored retirement plan, you are, in fact, taking advantage of this concept. Keep it up. Think about this – the stock markets declined nearly 50% the years following the 9/11 catastrophe. If you continued to fund your 401k, 403b, or other retirement plan during this downturn, you would have purchased twice as many shares. That's called a bargain!

"It's cheaper to hire an expert than to become one." —Anonymous

Here is an example of how dollar cost averaging can work to your benefit:

Dollar Cost Averaging

Month	Monthly Investment	Share Price	Shares Purchased
01	1,000.00	36.00	27.778
03	1,000.00	34.00	29.412
06	1,000.00	31.00	32.258
09	1,000.00	28.00	35.714
12	1,000.00	25.00	40.000
15	1,000.00	22.00	45.455
18	1,000.00	19.00	52.632
21	1,000.00	21.00	47.619
24	1,000.00	24.00	41.667
27	1,000.00	27.00	37.037
30	1,000.00	30.00	33.333
33	1,000.00	33.00	30.303
36	1,000.00	36.00	27.778
	36,000.00		1,358.90
		Current Share Price	X 36.00
			48,920.00
		Amount Invested	-36,000.00
		Profit	12,920.00
		Gain	35.5%

Principle #4: Use Professional Advice

For many investors, professional advice can make a big difference in the outcome of their investment returns. Going it alone, new investors can easily self-destruct because their tendency is to purchase a stock or mutual fund featured in a financial magazine. The problem with this is, by the time the publication gets into the hands of "mom and pop" investor, the investment may have already seen its best days. The first time investor usually buys high and dumps the investment the first time there is a downturn, thus — selling low. Buying low and selling high works much better!

The reality is that the novice investor will look for the "hot" fund (buying high), instead of looking for something that has been "ice cold" (out of favor) for the past couple of years (buying low) that may be ready for a turnaround. An example is buying pharmaceutical stocks after they went down 40-50% in 1992-94. Since then, many drug company stocks have more than tripled. Until the beginning investor perfects the investment process, they should use a professional financial advisor—preferably someone who has been in the business at least five to ten years. Let the "new kid on the block" practice on someone else—not you! Now, more than ever, money needs to be managed by a professional, not an amateur.

> ## Unlike the Lord, the market does not forgive those who know not what they do.
> ### —Warren Buffet

Consider this: At last count, there were:

- Over 40,000 companies trading stock worldwide
- Over 500 companies issuing bonds in the U.S.
- Over 11,000 companies issuing bonds worldwide
- Over 7,000 mutual funds
- Over 2,000,000,000 shares (on average) traded daily on the New York Stock Exchange

In my opinion, only a full-time professional with considerable experience can help navigate through the information overload.

> ## Information is everywhere — insight is not.
> ### —Anonymous

Be careful where you go for financial advice! Try this exercise sometime. Suppose you had $10,000 to invest. You walk into a bank for advice. What are they most likely to recommend? Probably a Certificate of Deposit. Walk down the street to an insurance agency. What are they most likely to recommend? Life insurance or an annuity. Walk down to the next block and walk into a brokerage firm. What will they suggest? Stocks, bonds, or mutual funds –– and probably their own mutual funds. Where is the objectivity? Whether you're age 25 or 65, whether you're worth $1,000 or $1,000,000, whether you want growth or safety—these institutions will generally offer everyone the same products. Try an independent financial planner. They don't just sell products. They put specific plans together and make specific recommendations based on your goals, risk tolerances, and personality. Be careful! Prescribing without proper diagnosis is malpractice and potentially deadly!

If Investing Were Easy, Then Everyone Would Be Rich – Everyone Is Not Rich.
—Nick Murray

Principle #5: Buy for the Long Term

Unless you are nearing the point of withdrawing your funds, it's better to have a long-term perspective, at least three to five years. Although prolonged bear (down) markets are a possibility, the variability of average annual returns over long periods of time is much less than over shorter periods. Patience helps the investor survive the ups and downs of the stock market. Sure, the market was up roughly two out of three years since 1900, but what about the down years? The market's down years averaged a negative 13% return—but the up years averaged a positive 22%. Also, the market has had back-to-back negative years only three times since World War II. What is the moral of the story? Over time, the positives have out-gained the negatives. Don't look at the "bumps in the road"–– keep an eye on your long-term goals.

When asked the secret to investing in the stock market, Peter Lynch, one of the greatest mutual fund managers of all time, responded —"not to get scared out of the market." John Templeton (a devout Christian who has given away millions of dollars, a true lighthouse on Wall Street), also one of the great portfolio managers of the past 50 years, is often asked what the secret is to his successful investing strategies. His answer— "Ignore fluctuations. Do not try to outguess the stock market. Buy a quality portfolio and invest for the long term."

Fear Is The Major Cause of Failure

Here are 72 "Reasons" not to invest:

1935 Spanish Civil War	1971 Wage & Price freeze
1936 Economy still struggling	1972 Largest trade deficit in U.S. history
1937 Recession	1973 Energy crisis
1938 War eminent in Europe, Asia	1974 Steepest market drop in 40 years
1939 War in Europe	1975 Clouded economic prospects
1940 France falls	1976 Economy slowly recovers
1941 Pearl Harbor	1977 Market slumps
1942 Wartime price controls	1978 Interest rates hike
1943 Industry mobilizes	1979 Oil skyrockets - 10% + unemployment
1944 Consumer goods shortage	1980 Interest rates hit all time high
1945 Post war recession predicted	1981 Deep recession begins - Reagan shot
1946 Dow tops 200 - "market too high"	1982 Worst recession in 40yrs. – debt crisis
1947 Cold War begins	1983 Market hits record - "market too high"
1948 Berlin Blockage	1984 Record federal deficits
1949 USSR explodes atomic bomb	1985 Economic growth slows
1950 Korean War	1986 Dow nears 2000 - "market too high"
1951 Excess Profits Tax	1987 the Crash - Black Friday
1952 U.S. seizes steel mills	1988 Fear of recession
1953 USSR explodes hydrogen bomb	1989 Junk bond collapse
1954 Dow tops 300 - "market too high"	1990 Gulf War/Worst 1yr. market. decline 6yrs.
1955 Eisenhower has heart attack	1991 Recession - "market too high"
1956 Suez Canal crisis	1992 Elections - market flat
1957 USSR launches Sputnik	1993 ???? No good reason!

1958 Recession	1994 Interest rates are going up
1959 Castro takes over Cuba	1995 The market is too high
1960 USSR downs U-2 spy plane	1996 I'll wait until after the elections
1961 Berlin Wall erected	1997 The Asian Crisis
1962 Cuban Missile crisis	1998 Clinton Crisis
1963 JFK assassinated	1999 Clinton Impeachment Hearings
1964 Gulf of Tonkin incident	2000 The Election Fiasco
1965 Civil rights marches	2001 World Trade Center
1966 Vietnam War escalates	2002 Middle East Crisis
1967 Newark race riots	2003 War in Iraq
1968 USS Pueblo seized, market too high	2004 Tsunami Disaster
1969 Money tightens, market falls	2005 Hurricane Katrina
1970 Conflict spreads to Cambodia	2006 Israel Lebanon Crisis

Stuff happens. Always has and always will. In spite of all the "stuff" that has taken place over the past 70+ years, a hypothetical $10,000 investment made on 12/31/34 in the Dow Jones Industrial Average was worth nearly $13,000,000 by the summer of 2006. That's thirteen million dollars (if you're having trouble with the multiple commas).

"For those properly prepared in advance, a bear market is not a calamity but an opportunity."
—Sir John Templeton

As the following chart illustrates, investing in the stock market can be a roller coaster ride, but it can also be rewarding. Remember, the only one who gets hurt on a roller coaster ride is the person who tries to get out.

*The Dow Jones Industrial Average is an unmanaged index that investors cannot invest into directly. The performance results of the DJIA are historical and are no indication of future performance. Investment returns and principal value will fluctuate, so that shares, when redeemed, may be worth more or less than the price you paid. *Source: Pioneer Funds Mutual Fund Illustrator Software, 5/02 & Yahoo Finance.*

The Long Ride

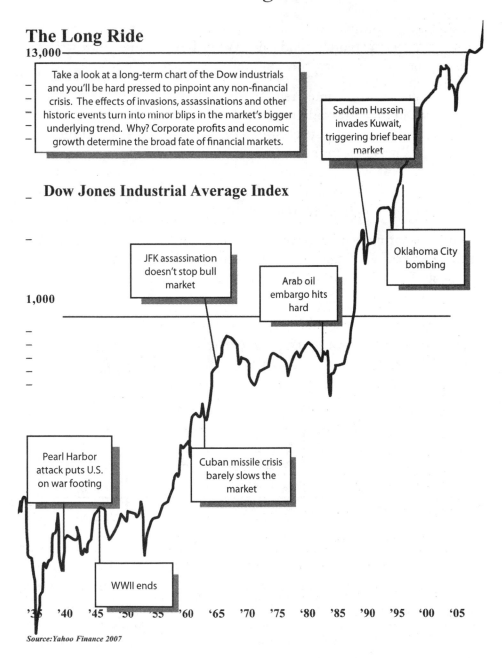

13,000

Take a look at a long-term chart of the Dow industrials and you'll be hard pressed to pinpoint any non-financial crisis. The effects of invasions, assassinations and other historic events turn into minor blips in the market's bigger underlying trend. Why? Corporate profits and economic growth determine the broad fate of financial markets.

Saddam Hussein invades Kuwait, triggering brief bear market

Dow Jones Industrial Average Index

JFK assassination doesn't stop bull market

Arab oil embargo hits hard

Oklahoma City bombing

1,000

Pearl Harbor attack puts U.S. on war footing

Cuban missile crisis barely slows the market

WWII ends

'35   '40   '45   '50   '55   '60   '65   '70   '75   '80   '85   '90   '95   '00   '05

Source: Yahoo Finance 2007

Whatever Happened to the Promised Land?

A recent Morningstar™ study showed that investors share in only 62% of the average mutual fund gain. Why? Because most inexperienced investors buy at the wrong time and sell at the wrong time.

Investors are sometimes tempted by the idea of getting out of the market just in time to avoid losses, then buying back in before it recovers. Long-term attempts to successfully time the market are futile. As appealing as it sounds in theory, executing a perfect exit from the market at its high — as well as an equally deft return at its trough – is almost impossible. This is because most market moves, either up or down, generally happen in brief spurts.

By attempting to time the market, you might just end up missing some of the market's best single-day performances. Sitting on the sidelines for as few as 10 of the market's best days could significantly cut into your investment returns.

TRYING TO TIME THE STOCK MARKET CAN BE COSTLY July 1, 1982 – July 29, 2007: A 25 Year History			
Growth of $10,000		Average Annual Total Returns	
Fully invested	⇢ 10.7%	⇢	$138,289
Miss the 10 best days	⇢ 9.4%	⇢	$104,541
Miss the 20 best days	⇢ 7.5%	⇢	$70,471
Miss the 30 best days	⇢ 52.0%	⇢	$45,196

Source: www.fivecentnickel.com. The stock market is represented by the Standard & Poor's 500 Index (S&P 500). The S&P 500 is a broad-based index, the performance of which is based on the performance of 500 widely held common stocks chosen for market size, liquidity and industry group representation. The index does not include any expenses, fees or charges. The index is unmanaged and should not be considered an investment.

"Our capital markets are simply a relocation center; they relocate the wealth from the impatient to the patient."
—Peter Lynch

Principle #6: Understanding the Importance of Compound Interest

Most people think a few extra percentage points of interest don't amount to much money. Not so! Understanding the value of compound interest is key to achieving financial freedom. The following chart shows what happens if you invest $100 per month at 5%, 8%, and 12% for 40 years (the amount of years we typically work):

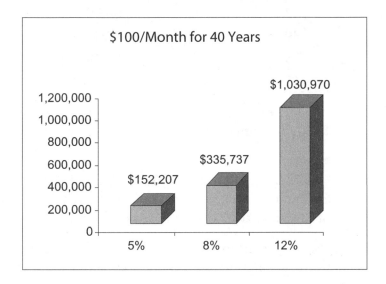

Get the point? By receiving a hypothetical 12% rate of return vs. 5%, you don't end up with 7% more money. In this case, it's 700% more money. It pays to invest wisely!

The Rule of 72 is another powerful illustration on the "magic" of compound interest. Divide the interest rate you are getting on your money into the number 72. The answer is the number of years it takes for your money to double. Let me illustrate. Take six percent, which is the current bank rate. Six divided into 72 is twelve. In other words, it will take twelve years for your money to double at six percent interest. Now –– suppose you could get a twelve percent rate of return. Twelve percent is just slightly less than what the Dow Jones Industrial Average has returned for the past 104 years. Twelve into seventy-two is six. It only takes six years for you to double your money at a 12% investment return.

Suppose a 25-year-old had $10,000 to invest:

Rule of 72

Age	6%	12%
25	10,000	10,000
31		20,000
37	20,000	40,000
43		80,000
39	40,000	160,000
55		320,000
61	80,000	640,000

This is a profound example of the difference between saving and investing — a $560,000 difference! It is also a great example of good stewardship.

Speaking of doubling... I'm often asked where the best place to invest is, and my standard answer is, "I'm particularly keen on Irish investments — it's because their capital is always Dublin."

We have the wrong definition of risk and safety. For example, if I put $5,000 in something, get $6,000 back, and it doesn't buy me what $5,000 used to buy me, then it's not safe.

Don't be left behind; get started today!
After all, Money Doesn't Take Care of Itself!

The following is an article I wrote for Leaders magazine, published in the fall of 2001. It outlines a common sense approach to investing versus the Internet frenzy in which so many people "lost their shirts," attempting to get rich quick. Enjoy!

"Hare" We Go Again
The Rabbit Dies – The Tortoise Wins

When the stock markets plummeted in 2001 from their highs of March of 2000, I was reminded of the story of the tortoise and the hare. I'm sure you are all familiar with the parable, so I won't bore you with the story here. (See your mother, if you need help.) The moral of the story, of course, is slow and steady generally wins – an unfocused and undisciplined approach usually doesn't!

The same can be true when it comes to investing. I sometimes go through the following exercise with potential clients who have unrealistic expectations. They want to go for the "home run" with no downside risk. (Adults do still believe in fairy tales.) This is hypothetical, of course, and is meant for illustrative purposes only.

Investor A (the hare) takes $100,000 and "goes for the gusto" by putting everything into the Technology Fund in 1999. Lo and behold, he is lucky enough to receive an 80% return on investment – not uncommon for technology funds that year. This aberration convinces Investor A that he is a genius and is ready to give up his day job. But wait! He wants to stay on the fast track and let it ride for another year. Year 2000 is less than kind, and the silly rabbit loses 40%.

Investor B (the tortoise) is happy with a target 12% average annual return through a diversified portfolio, i.e., bonds, cash, real estate investment trusts (REITs), and stocks (domestic and international). Investor B ends up with a 12% investment return in 1999 and 2000. After the two-year period, who is the winner? A or B? Most people answer "A". "If Investor A made 80% and then lost 40%, he is still up 40%. Investor B is only up 24%." WRONG! Let's do the math.

Investor A	Investor B
$100,000	$100,000
x 80% (1999)	x 12% (1999)
$180,000	$112,000
x -40% (2000)	x 12% (2000)
$108,000	$136,400
My example is hypothetical and for illustrative purposes only. It does not constitute a solicitation or guarantee.	

The dumb bunny finds out he is not a genius after all!

What is a reasonable expectation for investing in the stock market? The Dow Jones Industrial Average has averaged between 10-12% for the past 104 years. Over the past century, there have been both good and bad times – world wars, a depression, two stock market crashes, assassinations, several recessions, and various crises. What's the point? Bad things are always going to happen, and bad things will have a negative impact on the markets on a short-term basis. In spite of lots of bad things happening, the Dow has still averaged just shy of 12%. In my opinion, 12% is a reasonable expectation, not 30%, 40%, 50%, or 100%.

On the other hand, speculating can be very, very costly! Those looking for the big returns without weighing the downside are silly rabbits. Take a look at the following chart to see what you need to make back after a down year in order to break even:

Gaining It Back	
If you lose this much...	...You'll need to earn this much to break even
10%	11%
20%	25%
30%	43%
40%	67%
50%	100%
60%	150%
70%	233%
80%	400%
90%	900%
Source: USA TODAY research March 13, 2001	

The moral of the story? Stay away from "hare-brained schemes" – get back to basics! Once again, stick with the three golden rules of investing — Diversify, diversify, diversify!

Investing 101

Here is my final word on investing. After the events of 9/11 and the profound impact it had on the stock markets, I realized that many people do not have the staying power and stamina to ride out wild gyrations. If you got out of the market when it was down 50%, you would have lost half of your investment. If you held on until the markets recovered, you lost nothing. Too many people panicked and sold before the stock market recovered. If you are going to invest, "know thyself." Will you panic or will you stay the course? If you get sick on roller coasters, you may want to stay away from the stock market.

Chapter 7

Financial Planning 101

The following are the financial planning basics. Implement them yourself or hire a professional, such as an estate planner or financial planner, to help you put your plan together. It won't be easy, but it will be worth it!

#1 — Set Financial Goals

"Because, if you don't know where you're going,
you could wind up someplace else."
—Yogi Bearra

You should have financial goals, such as getting out of debt, retiring, buying a home, or putting children through college. Goals should be realistic and obtainable. They should be written and reviewed on a daily basis. When I was a quarter of a million in debt, my number one goal was to get out of debt. I had that goal and my other longer-term goals written on 3x5 index cards. I taped those cards on our refrigerator, medicine cabinet mirror, dashboard of my car, and to my desk. If you don't have your goals and objectives written where they can be seen on a regular basis, you will soon forget them and continue "chasing your tail till you're pushing up daisies." Just as the Lord told the Prophet Habakkuk to write the vision, you should also write your vision and goals. Reviewing written goals on a regular basis helps one to stay focused. Remember, nothing worthwhile in this life comes easy; you have to work hard to obtain it. Unfortunately, it's part of the curse. (Blame Adam and Eve!) Make sure you review your overall plan regularly and make adjustments as needed.

Remember — A Goal Is A Dream With a Deadline

Stay focused, and don't allow Job's "friends" to get you off course. There will be those who will try to distract and discourage you. Many so-called friends won't want you to succeed, because, if you do, it makes them look bad. When Nehemiah was busy rebuilding the wall around Jerusalem, his enemies continually tried to distract him from his mission. Nehemiah's reply was riveting – "I am doing a great work, so that I cannot come down (Nehemiah 6:3)." He was focused – you need to be the same.

Faith and Focus Will Work
When Blended with Persistence and Balance of Life
While Keeping God First

Keep in mind, Joseph had great dreams, but don't forget who tried to kill them... his own brothers!

#2 — Have a Written Budget

If you don't know what your net (after taxes) income is and what your expenses are on a monthly basis, it's almost impossible to be able to plan properly. When most people go through this exercise, they find they are spending more than they are taking home, which can't go on forever! Something has to give, usually your sanity. Larry Burkett developed excellent workbooks for the beginner budgeter, available at most Christian bookstores or at www.crown.org. As a reality check, you can go through your check ledger to see what you have spent on utilities, insurance, rent/mortgage, etc. for the past year. This way, you can determine if you are spending too much on any one category. As my wife and daughter used to say, "How can I be out of money? I still have checks left!".

If you find you're spending more than you're taking home each month, you only have three choices — 1) make more money, 2) spend less money, or 3) sell assets to raise money to pay off loans or debts. Don't buy things just because you can afford the monthly payments. It's more economical to save the money first and then pay cash for the item. You shouldn't be paying 12-18% interest on something that will be worthless in a couple of years anyway. Count the total cost of the item before you make the purchase. For instance, an item might have a sticker price of $1,000, but the store may offer 12 installment payments of $100 and your cost would be $1,200, plus tax.

I stopped buying things that weren't absolutely necessary, so I could get out of debt. First I asked myself, "How many hours would I have to work to buy this thing?" Then I would ask, "Was it worth it?" Most of the time, it was not. I got rid of all of my credit cards, except my American Express. On this credit card, you must pay the entire balance at the end of each month, or they will take it away. So, before I got into the checkout line, I needed to be sure I had the money to pay the charge card bill when it arrived. If you have balances on credit cards that charge interest, transfer the balance over to a 0% interest credit card (the offers you get in the mail every week). After you transfer the balances, cut up the old card (this is called "plastic" surgery) and work on paying off the balance you transferred to the 0% credit card.

#3 — Life Insurance

There has been a lot of controversy regarding life insurance over the years. In my opinion, most young couples, just starting out, should purchase term insurance. Term life insurance is the least expensive way to go. You can get the most coverage for the fewest dollars.

Whatever Happened to the Promised Land?

The purpose of life insurance is to replace lost income caused by a premature death. Let me use my wife and myself as an example. When we were married, back in 1976, we were each making around $30,000/year. We purchased our first home and wanted to protect each other if one of us died. Obviously, the mortgage payments would stay the same, but our household income would be cut in half. In all likelihood, whoever survived would have lost the house. So, we purchased a $250,000 term insurance policy on each other. If I were to die, my wife would get a tax-free check for $250,000. If she were to invest the proceeds properly, she could receive $30,000/year ($250,000 x 12% = $30,000/year) and never have to touch the principal. The insurance would replace my lost income. I recommend this strategy over paying off the house, because the lump sum you use to pay it off is lost forever. If you use this strategy, you'll eventually pay off your house and still have a "pot of money" from the life insurance proceeds.

Should a Christian own life insurance? Does owning life insurance show a lack of faith in God? I Timothy 5:8 states, *"But if anyone does not provide for his own, and especially for those of his household, he has denied the faith, and is worse than an unbeliever."* Not owning life insurance, if your family relies on your income, is just plain dumb! The last time I looked, the mortality rate in the United States was 100%. In other words, you are going to die. Make sure you take care of your family!

Other types of life insurance can be used for various other reasons. Variable Universal Life (VUL) is for high net worth individuals looking for tax-free retirement income. Whole life insurance is a dinosaur (in my opinion), and universal life is ideal for last-to-die policies in a life insurance trust, again for higher net worth individuals. Universal Life (UL), Whole Life (WL), and Variable Universal Life (VUL) insurance build cash value. Term insurance has no cash value but is generally much more inexpensive than UL, WL, or VUL. Although UL, WL, and VUL policies may sound more appealing than Term insurance, the reality is that, in most cases, upon your death, the insurance company keeps the cash value in these types of policies. In other words, if you own a $25,000 cash value policy and you die, your beneficiary receives the $25,000 death benefit, not $25,000 plus the cash value. You lose the cash value! Buy inexpensive Term life insurance, and invest the difference of what you would have spent on a cash value policy into a mutual fund or some other investment vehicle. Instead of the insurance company keeping your cash value, your heirs receive your investment.

Financial Planning 101

You could have 100 life insurance agents in a room and not get any two to agree on which type of policy is the best. This section is to give my perspective, as a financial planner, on life insurance. (The other 99 agents can write their own books.) If your life insurance policies are 20-25 years old, consider upgrading to a newer policy. Here are seven good reasons to do so...

1. The cost of insurance has decreased by 50-60% over the past 50 years due to increased competition and our longer life expectancies. So, you may be able to reduce your premium payments or increase your death benefit, depending on a variety of factors.

2. Interest rates in newer Universal Life contracts are generally higher than the old Whole Life policies, which is typically 4%.

3. Many newer policies offer living benefits, allowing you to use money from the death benefit while you're still living to pay for nursing home costs, medical expenses, or in-home nursing care -- on a tax-free basis.

4. You can direct the insurance company to invest your cash value in the stock market, bond market, or in money markets.

5. You can choose Option 2, where the beneficiary receives the death benefit and the cash value, not just the death benefit like most older Whole Life policies.

6. Some insurance companies allow you to make tax-free and interest-free loans on many newer policies.

7. In almost all cases, the insured is the owner of their policy. From an estate planning point of view, this is a "no, no". To potentially avoid estate taxes, make sure someone other than the insured person owns the policy.

It has been my experience that most people are "sold" life insurance policies and, for the most part, do not fully understand them. After the sale, the contracts are thrown in a drawer or safety deposit box and left there until death. I'm not sure if it's a lack of understanding or the lack of fortitude to let another life insurance agent back in the house. For whatever the reason, old life insurance policies become "sacred cows." Not considering upgrading a 40-year-old policy is like not upgrading a 40-year-old black & white television to a color television.

What's the cost? Generally nothing. Here are two examples of real clients who upgraded:

Example 1

Life Insurance Proposal Female Age 55 Smoker	
Existing Coverage	Existing Cost Per Year
$6,500	$231.71 for life
Existing Cash Value $2,206.02	
Proposed Coverage	Proposed Cost Per Year
$10,000	-0-

Example 2

Life Insurance Proposal Male Age 68 Non-Smoker	
Existing Coverage	Existing Cost Per Year
$15,000	-0-
Existing Cash Value $11,877.54	
Proposed Coverage	Proposed Cost Per Year
$31,000	-0-

In both examples, the policies were several years old. There were no surrender charges or penalties to the insured.

Any tax consequences for upgrading your policy? Not if it is done correctly. The IRS allows policy owners to exchange older policies to newer ones through Section 1035 of the IRS Code on a tax-free basis. The rules governing 1035 exchanges can be complex.

Should everyone consider upgrading? No! If you are unhealthy and uninsurable, DO NOT cancel your older policies. Something is better than nothing. Another reason for not upgrading is the suicide contestability clause. The two-year contestability clause precludes the insurance company from paying the death claim due to suicide.

As a final thought, if you don't feel you need life insurance at your stage in life and you have a substantial amount of cash value in your older policy, the IRS does allow you to make 1035 exchange (tax-free) your cash value to an annuity. These are tax-deferred investment and savings vehicles. You may (if you don't die prematurely) accumulate more value over time in an annuity than in your life insurance policy death benefit. This is, of course, a gamble. (If you die soon after making an exchange, your beneficiaries would receive no life insurance benefit, only the annuity value.) If you feel you don't need the coverage, and if you're tired of paying premiums, and if you have accumulated enough wealth to take care of all the things that need to be taken care of when you're gone, then consider exchanging the cash value to an annuity.

#4 — Set Up An Estate Plan

"A good man leaveth an inheritance to his children's children."
(Proverbs 13:22)

Whether you're worth ten thousand or ten million dollars, you should have an estate plan. For those with estates of under one million dollars, the basic tools include a will, power of attorney, and living will.

A. A Will: A Will tells the probate Judge how you want your "worldly goods" to be distributed upon your death. If you don't have a Will, the Judge has to guess on how you wanted your estate to be given away, which can create a variety of problems. The Judge may not distribute your estate the way you wanted it to be distributed. In the state of Connecticut (where I live), if a spouse were to die without a will, the surviving spouse would receive 50% of the deceased's estate, and the children would split the remaining 50%. That's probably not the way the deceased would have wanted it.

Let me share a true story of one of my clients. Mr. & Mrs. Smith (the names have been changed to protect the guilty) had an estate of $500,000. It was a second marriage for both. Mr. Smith had two adult children from his previous marriage, and Mrs. Smith had a grown daughter from her first marriage. They owned three homes, their primary residence and two investment properties. Mr. Smith was a self-employed plumber. They were doing better than "okay." Each year, when they would come in for their review, I would ask them if they had taken care of getting a will.

Whatever Happened to the Promised Land?

Each year I would get the same answer — "We'll get to it." A couple of summers ago, while driving to their vacation destination, Mrs. Smith fell asleep behind the wheel of the car. Mr. Smith was killed instantly. Mrs. Smith survived.

Settling the estate was a nightmare. With no will, the three children were to receive 50% of Mr. Smith's estate, and Mrs. Smith was entitled to the remaining 50% — not what Mr. Smith had in mind. How do you split three homes between four heirs equally? No one could agree on who was to get what, so the judge ordered all properties to be sold — at discount prices, I might add. (Housing prices had just hit a ten year low in Connecticut.) After all the homes were sold, the money was divided. Mrs. Smith received half, and the three children divided the other half. Mrs. Smith had nowhere to live and had no income coming in, since she wasn't a plumber. All it would have taken to avoid this mess was a couple of hours with an attorney and a couple hundred dollars to set up a will.

Another very important reason to have a will is naming a guardian for minor children. If both the husband and wife were to die at the same time, without a will, the probate judge would be forced to decide where the children were to live and who would care for them. Since the judge doesn't know you, your children, or your family members, he or she would probably not make the best decisions. In some cases, your children may not end up with a relative but in a foster home. In some extreme cases, your children may not end up in the same household. Make sure you have an up-to-date, legal, binding will!

B. Durable Power of Attorney (POA): A Durable Power of Attorney is a legal document that allows someone to transact someone else's business, financial or otherwise, when one is incapacitated or unavailable. Let me give a couple of examples of how POAs come in handy.

An elderly couple (clients of mine) wanted to sell their home and move to Florida. The weather and economy were the main reasons they wanted to get out of the Northeast. They put their house up for sale and had a qualified buyer within a couple of months. Just prior to the closing, the husband was diagnosed with Alzheimer's disease. This rendered him legally incompetent; he could no longer sign the necessary documents for the closing. The wife had to petition the court to get the necessary approval to sign for her husband. This takes time and money, and they could have potentially lost the buyer while all this legal maneuvering was taking place.

Mr. & Mrs. Jones (also clients of mine) were retired and middle class. They had enough to get by. You might say they were fairly typical of a 70-year-old couple. Mrs. Jones had stayed home to raise the three children, and Mr. Jones worked at the same company for most of his life. So, all of the couple's retirement money was in Mr. Jones' name. Mrs. Jones called me not too long ago to tell me that Mr. Jones was in the hospital. The initial diagnosis was dementia. He is now, of course, legally incapacitated. With a durable POA, Mrs. Jones was able to sign legal documents for Mr. Jones and do some last minute (legal) maneuvering of assets before Mr. Jones was put into a nursing home. This saved Mrs. Jones tens of thousands of dollars that would have been taken by the convalescent home.

If only one spouse is still living, then they should consider giving durable POA to a child or sibling. The durable POA can be set up to be used only when someone is incapacitated or on an ongoing basis, or if an elder, competent person needs help with their affairs.

C. A Living Will: A living will is a necessity! It is a separate and distinct document from the will. The living will is your instruction to your health care provider if you are terminally ill or comatose and have no hope of recovering. It tells your family if you want the "plug pulled" or not. Your doctor or family cannot make that decision for you. It must be in writing. I had a client, Joyce, whose elderly mother went into a coma. Joyce and her sister were discussing mom's options with the doctor. The physician clearly stated there was no hope. Joyce instructed the doctor to take mom off life support. That's what mom had instructed her to do. Joyce's sister immediately responded, "You're not killing my mother." First of all, the doctor was unable to carry out Joyce's instructions because mom's wishes were not in writing. Secondly, the fact that mom did not have a living will created strife in the family. Lastly, you could end up in court with a judge making these kinds of decisions, and he/she doesn't even know the family.

I had a distant relative who developed a rare form of cancer. There was clearly no hope. She went into a coma for months before passing away. Unfortunately for her husband, she had used up all of her medical insurance benefits. When she died, the hospital sued the husband for the remaining medical bills. They foreclosed on the home in their joint names and attached his wages. He was forced to move into a one room rental and died shortly thereafter of a massive heart attack. I still say to this day — he died of a broken heart. A living will would have prevented this catastrophe. You owe it to your family to take care of these very important documents. Most estate planning attorneys don't "bite," and it's worth the few hundred dollars on the front end to provide proper planning for your loved ones. As the TV commercial says, "You can pay me now or you can pay me later."

For those with an estate over one million dollars, you will need to take advantage of additional estate planning tools. At the time of publication, anyone with an estate greater than one million dollars will have to pay federal (and possibly state) estate taxes. Those taxes can be as high as 55%. By setting up a living trust, sometimes referred to as a marital trust or A-B trust, you can legally avoid nearly $200,000 in estate taxes! If your estate is over the one million dollar threshold and you don't set up a trust, you are unnecessarily giving your money to the IRS instead of your loved ones. Trusts can potentially help your estate bypass probate. Trusts are far too complicated to deal with in this book. The Economic Growth and Tax Relief Reconciliation Act of 2001 has complicated estate planning almost beyond comprehension. Consider the following quote from the August, 2001 issue of *Kiplinger's*:

> "Congress did vote to repeal the estate tax. But don't hold your breath or you will expire long before it takes full effect. The amount that you can leave tax-free to your heirs will rise from $675,000 this year to $1 million in 2002, and ultimately to $3.5 million in 2009. The top estate tax rate – now 55% on estates larger than $3 million – will fall to 50% next year and gradually decline to 45% in 2007. In 2010, the estate tax disappears. But it comes back to life for those who die in 2011 and later, with a $1 million tax-free transfer limit and a top rate of 55%."

I'm sure that's about as clear as mud. (Now you know why the opposite of progress is Congress!) The bottom line – if your estate is sizable, get professional help from an estate planning attorney.

There are dozens of books published on the subject of estate planning. Check out your local bookstore or call an estate planning attorney. They specialize in trusts and can be far more helpful than I can be.

A final consideration — most people don't realize there are several layers of taxes due upon death on tax-qualified money. Qualified money, such as a 401(k), IRA, retirement plan, or 403B, is money you have not paid taxes on. When the first spouse dies, all qualified money can be rolled over to the surviving spouse with no taxes due. However, when the second spouse dies, all kinds of taxes are due — federal income taxes, state income taxes, probate, federal estate taxes, and state succession taxes. That's potentially five taxes totaling as much as 70-80%! To avoid making your rich Uncle Sam even richer, consider spending down your IRAs or retirement funds before you're forced to at age 70½, or think about a life insurance trust. Again, this is much too complicated to explain in detail here. The bottom line is that a life insurance trust will 1) allow tax-free withdrawal out of your estate, and 2) potentially give a large amount to your heirs, completely tax-free, avoiding the five taxes totaling up to 70-80%. As my estate planning attorney says, "The only two reasons you don't need to do an estate plan are 1) if you're not going to die, or 2) if you don't own anything."

Do Your Family a Favor

As I said earlier, the mortality rate in the United States is 100%. Put another way – we are all going to die (like it or not). Do your family a favor and keep good financial records. I got a call from my grandmother in Ohio one afternoon to let me know that my grandfather had just passed away. She went on to say, "Richard, you'll need to come out here and help me. I don't know if I'm rich or if I'm poor." For the most part, my grandfather took care of the finances. It took me three solid weeks of going through my grandfather's "stuff" to sort out everything for my grandmother. If it was difficult for me, I couldn't begin to imagine how difficult it would be for a layman. Since it's impossible to ask a dead person questions regarding his or her finances, it's critical to keep your family informed while you're alive.

This event motivated me to update my financial statement and financial records every six months for my wife. You should let your beneficiary know what you own, the account numbers, who the agent or company is that you invested with and where to find the "stuff," such as certificates of deposit or stock certificates. Telephone numbers and addresses of the financial institutions are also helpful. This should be done in writing and updated often (at least annually). It will save a lot of heartache. No one wants to deal with these issues while grieving. Let me go so far as to recommend you plan your own funeral. It takes so much pressure off your loved ones.

I saw the anguish my grandmother went through. She was forced to make so many decisions while under duress. When I got home, I immediately set up an appointment with our local funeral director and planned my funeral, including picking out all the necessary items, so my wife would not be forced into going through this process while grieving. It may sound morbid to you, but think of how your loved ones will feel if you don't take my advice!

I was helping a couple with their estate planning and they started to have this discussion. The husband turns to his wife and asks if she would want to continue to live in their house if he died. She said sure she wanted to stay there forever. So, he asked her if she were to get remarried would her new husband also live in the house? She replied if she did get remarried her new husband would live there too. So he asked about his car, his prized Corvette, would she let him drive the car? She said if he needed to drive the car, he could drive it. Taken aback by the way the conversation was going, the husband prepared himself to ask her the really big question; what about his golf clubs? She wouldn't let him use those, would she? She said no, absolutely not! He's left-handed!

This is what you should do before you go to bed tonight:

1. Make a list of all assets.
2. Make a list of all liabilities.
3. Make a list of all insurance.
4. Make sure all beneficiary information is up-to-date.
5. Make a list of all group benefits from your job and/or from the military.
6. Make a list of what gifts or bequeaths you want to make.
7. Make sure any final wishes or instructions are in writing, witnessed, and notarized.

See you in the morning!

#5 — Pay Down Your Debt

As my daughter, Jennifer, says, "Debt is growth's biggest enemy." If you have a mortgage, credit card debt, car payments, or consumer loans, you are paying an additional 6-18% annually versus paying cash, just for the "luxury" of paying in installments. Obviously, most people cannot pay cash to purchase a home, but I will show you how to pay the house off sooner than later in this section. As I have mentioned several times before (please forgive me), I had debts totaling $250,000. I wanted desperately to pay everyone. Not wanting to file for bankruptcy, I contacted each company to which I was indebted. I explained my predicament (a humbling experience) and told them I wanted to start a repayment schedule. Each company accepted different amounts, from $5 to $100 per month.

The bottom line was that each company worked with me. I prioritized my debt and made a list of everyone to whom I owed money. Those charging the highest percentage rates were on the top of the list, and the lowest rates were at the bottom. The list was five full pages. The exercise was depressing, to say the least. I taped page one to our refrigerator to constantly remind me of my commitment and started to write out the checks, as I was able. If any extra money came in, such as a tax refund, birthday money or Christmas cash, I would pay extra on the debt highest on the list. Believe it or not, it took us 18 months to pay off number one on the list. I then took the money I was paying toward number one and applied it to number two on the list, which took just six months to pay off. I then took the money I was paying toward numbers one and two, plus any extra income, and applied it towards number three, and so on.

It was extremely satisfying to cross off the last bill eight years later. When all the debts on the list were paid, I took the extra cash flow and paid off the cars. Once the cars were paid off, I went after the mortgage. It took seven more years, but I was completely debt-free.

Did you ever take the time to calculate how much your house will cost you? Take your monthly mortgage payment times the number of payments you'll make. The total is usually 2.5-3 times the actual purchase price of your home. That's a total cost of $300,000 paid on a $100,000 home! The first time I did the math, I felt ill. I strongly suggest you pay down your mortgage sooner. In other words, make extra payments or increase your monthly payment. Your mortgage company or bank will not refuse your money. If your payment is $830/month, make it $900 or $1,000 when and if you can. It makes a huge difference. One hundred extra dollars per month paid towards your principal can shorten a 30-year mortgage by almost seven years! Can't afford an extra $100/month? Try using your tax refund, Christmas bonus, or birthday money. (Most of us blow our extra money on depreciating assets or "toys" anyway.) Imagine the peace of mind of not having a monthly mortgage payment! Good stewardship now pays big dividends later!

A word of caution – most CPA's and tax advisors do not recommend paying off your mortgage early because you lose the tax deduction. I never understood the logic. If you spent a dollar on your mortgage interest, and you got 27% back on your tax return as a deduction, your net benefit was 27 cents. On the other hand, if you earned a dollar and paid the income taxes on that dollar, at 27% with no tax deduction, your net is 73 cents. Which would you rather have in your pocket, 27 cents or 73 cents?

What could you do with all of the extra monthly income if you had no bills to pay? Anything you wanted! Being debt-free and financially independent is joy unspeakable. It's ten thousand times better than you think it will be! A final piece of advice — when I finished paying off our last car payment, I took the monthly car payment and saved it. By the time we needed a newer car, I was able to pay cash instead of starting car payments all over again with all that nasty interest. Also, never buy a new car. You can buy a pre-owned, fully warranted, two- to three-year-old car for nearly half the price of a new car. New cars lose too much value as soon as you drive them off the lot. "Living life to its credit limit" should not be our personal motto.

It's Not Hard To Meet Expenses — They Are Everywhere

#6 — Start an Emergency Fund

Emergencies will come; things happen. Cars and furnaces break down, relatives die in other parts of the world, jobs are lost, etc. My suggestion is $5,000-$10,000 put aside in a savings account, credit union, or a money market fund for a single person ($20,000-$25,000 for a married couple). Make sure you can readily access the funds via ATM, debit card, or a checkbook. It is wise to have an emergency fund, although I have yet to meet anyone with a $25,000 emergency. (Of course, you'll only have the need if you aren't prepared.)

#7 — Save for Retirement

Although retirement isn't biblical (unless you're a Levite), you'll probably want to take it easy and slow down someday. Social security accounts for only about 20-50% of the income most retirees need to live comfortably — a large part depends on where you live. Where will you make up the difference — work part time, reduce your lifestyle, or move?

The best solution is to save for retirement as soon as possible. Take advantage of your company-sponsored retirement plan, if available. (See next section "Reduce your Taxes" Section B.) Also consider opening a Roth IRA. Roths became law in 1998. They now allow individuals to put $5,000/year away ($6,000 if you are over age 50 and twice as much for couples), as long as you are still working (subject to certain income limitations). The advantage of a Roth IRA is that your money grows tax-free and can be taken out tax-free if left for five years and you're over age 59½. The money can also be withdrawn (up to $10,000) for education or first time home buyers without taxes or penalties, even if you're under age 59½.

The following examples profoundly illustrate the benefits of tax-free compounding in a Roth IRA:

$6,000/year X 12%** X 10 years = $117,927

(You pay zero taxes on the gain of $57,927.)

$6,000/year X 12%** X 20 years = $484,192

(You pay zero taxes on the gain of $364,192.)

By all means, take advantage of this wonderful retirement plan!

**Assumed interest rate/rate of return - For Illustration Purposes Only

Once you have exhausted all other options, start saving in annuities. They are tax-deferred retirement plans (age 59½ restrictions) and come in all shapes and sizes. Do your homework before committing your assets to something long-term.

My final idea for retirement planning is — You can ask your spouse to continue to work while you retire — although this idea rarely goes over well and can cause division and strife in the home. I wonder why!

#8 — Reduce Your Taxes

> The legal right of a tax payer to decrease the amount of what otherwise would be his taxes, or altogether avoid them, by means which the law permits, cannot be doubted.
> —Justice Sutherland

The average American works two hours and 46 minutes of each eight-hour workday to pay federal, state, and local taxes[1]. (I learned how to beat the system; I take off the first three hours of each workday.) We pay taxes on what we earn, we pay taxes on what we save, we pay taxes on what we spend, and we pay taxes when we die. If you feel as if you're paying more than your fair share, here are five strategies to help lighten Uncle Sam's "take."

A. Make a charitable contribution before 12/31. While gifts of cash are the most typical method of giving (and most welcomed), donating appreciated assets instead of cash will give you a greater tax break. Not only do you get the tax deduction for the gift, you avoid the capital gains tax that otherwise would have been due. For example, suppose you bought $5,000 of IBM stock a few years ago, and it is now worth $10,000. Also, suppose you wanted to make a $10,000 donation or pay your tithes for the next couple of years. Instead of writing out a check, why not donate the IBM stock to your church or favorite charity! Believe me, they would love to have it! They can then sell the stock and pay no taxes. You get a $10,000 tax deduction, and you avoid paying the capital gains tax on the growth –– a double tax break for you! Additionally, there is nothing stopping you from taking your $10,000 in cash that you were going to give away and repurchase IBM. You now have the new higher cost basis. I like to call it "disappearing capital gains." Everyone comes out ahead, except your "uncle" in D.C.

This concept also works on real estate and life insurance. As many of us get older, we may have a reduced need for life insurance. Why not convert your cash value policies to paid up policies, and donate them to your church or favorite charity. They can cash them in, and, again, you get a double tax break – 1) a tax deduction on the amount (cash value) contributed, and 2) you escape the taxes on the gain or appreciation.[2]

B. Take advantage of your employer-sponsored retirement plan. The 401(k) offered by many large corporations will allow employees to contribute a percentage of their income, up to certain limitations, pretax, and most corporations will match what you contribute. It is astounding how many employees do not take advantage of the free money offered by their companies! For example, suppose you put away $1,000/year into the 401(k) plan (less than $20/week). The first benefit to you is that the $1,000 is deducted from your gross income. In other words, you do not pay income taxes on that money. If you are in a 27% tax bracket, you'll save $270 in taxes.

Put another way, it will only cost you $730 to put away $1,000. In addition, if your employer matches your contribution (dollar for dollar), it only costs you $730 to put away $2,000.3 Remember, "free" is generally good! Not all companies offer the same kind of retirement plans. Non-profit organizations should offer 403(b) plans. Smaller companies may offer profit sharing plans, simple plans, or Simplified Employee Pension (SEP) plans. Ask your boss or Human Resources Department. I haven't found too many legitimate reasons for not saving for retirement, especially in light of the tax breaks and potential free money.

C. Keep your investments as tax efficient as possible. For every dollar interest you make, remember the tax consequences. For the average American, that's around 30%, between state, federal, and city taxes. You have no doubt heard of the 80/20 Rule. Well, this is the 70/30 Rule. The "tax man" gets 30%; you get the rest. What a deal for you-know-who! What about those taxes on dividends and capital gains doled out by mutual funds? According to The Boston Sunday Globe (3/14/99 issue), the estimated tax bill for mutual fund investors was expected to top $40 billion in 1999. Let's say you invested $100,000 into a fund on January 2, 1999. At the end of the year, you have $112,000 — that's a pretax total return of 12%. However, if $10,000 of the growth was generated from short-term capital gains, you'll likely pay $3,000 or more in taxes. That lowers your after-tax return to $7,000 or 7%. It's not what you earn that matters, it's what you keep!

Whatever Happened to the Promised Land?

A tax-efficient investment is one that could be expected to produce favorable tax consequences. There are several types of tax-efficient investments:

- Tax-free. Income from municipal bond funds may be free from federal, state and sometimes city taxes, which can be advantageous for individuals in higher tax brackets. Municipal bonds typically represent an excellent value for those paying a lot of taxes, and sometimes even those in lower tax brackets get better after-tax yield (relative to treasuries or corporate bonds).

- Index funds are tax-efficient. An index fund seeks investment results that mirror the price and yield of a major stock or bond index, such as the Standard & Poors (S&P) 500 Index. These types of funds employ a passive management strategy designed to track the performance of an index and, therefore, have little or no turnover (buying and selling), which results in virtually no taxes until you sell. If you like unmanaged funds, this is an option also.

- Tax managed mutual funds. Tax managed mutual funds seek to achieve strong after-tax returns by managing investments to provide long-term growth and reduce taxes.

- Tax-deferred annuities. Variable and fixed annuities reduce current taxes through tax deferred compounding. In fact, they offer triple compounding. Triple compounding means you make interest on your principal, interest on interest, and interest on the tax savings. In other words, the money normally withdrawn to pay taxes each year remains in the annuity to compound. Take a look at the following chart to see what interest rate you would have to receive from a taxable investment to equal a tax-deferred annuity.

Tax-Deferred Yield Equivalency				
Tax-Deferred Yield of:	5%	6%	7%	8%
Equals a taxable yield of:				
Tax Bracket:				
15%	5.9%	7.1%	8.2%	9.4%
28%	6.9%	8.3%	9.7%	11.1%
31%	7.2%	8.7%	10.1%	11.6%
This chart is for illustration purposes only. No future taxes or surrender charges are considered.				

Without getting overly complicated, not only can you defer taxes, but also you can potentially withdraw up to 80% tax-free from annuities by utilizing what is called the exclusion ratio. Again, talk to an expert to see if these investment options are right for you and your family.

April 15th is not the time to think about taxes. You should be thinking about taxes before making an investment purchase.

Taxman

Let me tell you how it will be
There's one for you, nineteen for me
'Cause I'm the taxman.

Should five percent appear too small
Be thankful I don't take it all
'Cause I'm the taxman.

If you drive a car, I'll tax the street,
If you try to sit, I'll tax your seat.
If you get too cold, I'll tax the heat,
If you take a walk, I'll tax your feet.

Don't ask me what I want it for
If you don't want to pay some more
'Cause I'm the taxman.

—The Beatles

D. Charitable Remainder Trust (CRT). You've done a good job of accumulating a sizable estate. Perhaps you have real estate, stocks, bonds, and/or a business. As I have already stated, you may be facing income taxes, capital gains tax, sales tax, property taxes, and estate taxes up to 70-80% — it's the curse of a good economy. A CRT may be the solution to your tax problems. It not only can provide greater income to you and your heirs, but also to your favorite charities. A CRT is a tax-exempt trust designed to pay you a stream of income for life or a term of years. At the termination of the trust, the assets that remain are paid to the charities of your choice. Consider the following benefits:

- No capital gains tax. Once your assets are in a trust, you'll incur no capital gains tax when you decide to sell your assets.

- Reduced income tax. Because you name a favorite charity or charities as the recipient of the present value of the remainder interest upon your death, you are eligible for an income tax deduction at the time you transfer your assets into a CRT.

- Potentially more income. You've saved both capital gains and income tax by transferring your assets to a CRT. That gives you more capital to invest and potentially more income, depending upon the success of your investment.

- More for your loved ones. You can use your income and tax savings from your CRT to contribute to a wealth replacement trust (an irrevocable life insurance trust) for your heirs. The proceeds from this trust pass to your heirs tax-free. Any remainder in your CRT is paid to your selected charities upon the termination of the trust.

Here is an example of a CRT in action:

A 75-year-old couple came in for a financial plan. They had $80,000 in Pfizer stock with a very low cost basis. (They paid approximately $20,000.) Pfizer's dividend yield was around 2% at the time. The couple donated the stock to charity; they got an immediate tax deduction of $80,000. The stock was sold by the charity, so no taxes on the gain were owed. The money was reinvested in a higher yielding investment. Our couple is now receiving 6% income instead of 2%. When the couple passes away, the charity keeps the $80,000 investment.

While we are on the subject, here's a final thought on estate planning. If you're planning to leave money to your church or charity when you pass away, consider naming them as the beneficiary on your IRA, 401(k), or retirement plan. This will save the income tax your heirs would otherwise have to pay on it. Give your heirs "regular" or non-qualified money (money you have already paid taxes on). It won't make any difference to your charity — they don't pay taxes, but your heirs will.

E. Make Less Money. This is my least favorite strategy. I use strategies A-D; it's good stewardship.

As stewards of capital, we can give it away, spend it, invest it, hoard it, waste it, or give it to the IRS — it's your choice!

#9 — College Planning for Children

The last calculation I did for a young couple with a newborn child was that they would need to save $320/month for 18 years (assuming a 12% hypothetical return) to be able to pay for the child's college education. After I "picked them up off the floor," I explained their other options.

Option #1: The government will allow any U.S. citizen, who is current with their income taxes and who has no prior drug conviction, to borrow 100% of the cost of college (no matter what your income is) through the Sallie Mae organization. These are low interest, (and in most cases) tax-deductible loans. Many parents are also eligible for tax credits for a portion of the tuition paid. With tax credits, you get back some of your college expenses when you file your income tax return.

Option #2: You can take a home equity loan, if needed, which (in most cases) is also tax-deductible. Remember, I am not in favor of taking on debt. This is a last resort. There are also grants and scholarships, and you can pray that your kids become gifted students or athletes.

Don't do what some of our family members did — nothing. We were at a family outing several years ago. My uncle just declared that he had started working a second full-time job to be able to pay for his oldest daughter's college costs. I joked with him and asked if he intended to work a third full-time job with his son starting college in two years. Two years later, we went to the same family outing and found out my aunt had started a second job to help pay for the younger son's college costs.

Getting back to my young couple with the newborn — since they couldn't afford $320/month, I suggested starting with $100/month and making additional contributions when the child received money for a birthday or Christmas, etc. I also suggested increasing the $100/month contribution to $150 or $200/month the next time either parent got a raise and continue to do so until they made up for lost time. They thought this to be a reasonable approach. You should save for retirement before saving for college. If forced to, you can borrow money for college; you cannot borrow money to retire.

Did you hear about the banking executive who was arrested for embezzling $100,000 to pay for his son's college education?

"I have just one question for you," his attorney quipped. "Where were you planning to get the rest of the money?"

The following is a reprint of an article I wrote on college planning. I hope it helps you to understand the process a little better.

How I Got Uncle Sam to Pay for My Son's College Tuition — At NO COST to Me!

There I was — a proud father, writing out the first college tuition check ($10,000) for my son. The reason for the sense of pride? I had the foresight to start saving 15 years earlier!

I have been a financial planner for 15 years, and I am also my best client. I opened a Uniform Gifts to Minor Account (UGMA) when I first started in the industry. My son, Shawn, was just three years old then. I didn't have a lot of money — a young family, new home, new career — and could only afford $100/month back in 1984. Right after the stock market crash of 1987, I was able to increase my contribution to $200/month. (I love a bargain. Buy low; sell high!) A few years later, I increased it again to $250/month. "Fast forwarding" to my son's high school graduation, we had $80,000 in the UGMA account. Ironically, his annual college tuition payment was $20,000.

At this point, a strong bull market and 15 years of dollar cost averaging (systematically investing through the ups and downs) into a couple of good mutual funds made me look like a financial genius (or just plain lucky)! Either way, I was able to write out $10,000 checks for eight semesters, and Shawn would end up with any appreciation on his mutual fund UGMA over the next four years as a graduation present!

Proper planning does pay off. However, when I sat down to write that first check, I heard a "voice" saying, "Are you nuts?" (Those who know me already know the answer.) Over the past few months, I had read a couple of articles in trade journals and remembered the cheap cost of borrowing money for college tuition. It was approximately 7%* and tax deductible for many, which can net out to be less than 5% for numerous taxpayers. I had been averaging slightly over 15% per year in Shawn's UGMA account, and much of the growth was not taxed.

(*There are additional incentives to potentially reduce the rates even lower.)

After researching and "crunching" some numbers, I determined I was "nuts" to pay for my son's tuition. I realized I could borrow 100% of the tuition at substantially lower rates than I was earning on his two mutual fund accounts.

My son and I can borrow $80,000 at a cost of 5% net after taxes. Hopefully, I can continue to compound my son's money at a substantially higher, after-tax return. (I realize I didn't discover the "meaning of life" here, but it was a tremendous revelation to me.) I realized Shawn could borrow a total of $17,125 through the Federal Stafford Loan Program. He doesn't make any repayments until six months after graduation and can take up to ten additional years to pay it off. The monthly payment in 4.5 years is only $208 for ten years. I can borrow the rest ($62,875) over a four-year period. My payments start right after each semester's check is paid to the college.

This is where my illustration gets a little crazy. Remember, I was paying $250/month into Shawn's UGMA for years. Additionally, he had been in private school from kindergarten through high school, and I was used to paying a monthly tuition payment of

$500. My rationale was to pick up the monthly payments for each semester's loan as he progressed through college out of my pocket. After his freshman year, my monthly payment is only $268, a far cry from the $750/month I was contributing to his private education and UGMA. (My wife and I have some extra spending money after all of those years!)

If Shawn's UGMA continues to grow as it has in the past (and I firmly believe it will), his $80,000 will double six months after graduation, when he has to start repaying his portion of the loans. After he graduates, I will give him his mutual fund accounts ($160,000) and the balance of the loans to pay off. He then can do a couple of things:

1. Pay off the entire loan balance of approximately $60,000. (Remember, I have been making payments on my portion of the loan for 4.5 years.) He now has $100,000 left, after paying off the entire loan balance. How much would he have if I paid for his tuition from his UGMA starting year one? Certainly not $100,000! He could start a business, make a substantial down payment on a home, or subsidize his income while getting started in the "real world." Not a bad graduation present!

2. Set up a systematic withdrawal plan on the $160,000 of approximately $1,000/month to pay off the loans over time and still have his money grow slightly. By the time all of the loans are paid off, he could theoretically have $175,000.

WOW! You've got to love this country! Uncle Sam picks up the tuition payments while my son's money continues to grow. Shawn makes the world a better place to live, and I am the proud father!

The moral of the story: Next time you hear a voice in your head, either get professional help or listen carefully!

—Financial Service Advisors
July/August 2000

Here are the options available for funding your child's education:

1. Uniform Gifts to Minor Act (UGMA) - UGMAs are an effective vehicle to shift money out of a parent's name and have it taxed at a child's lower tax bracket. The parent controls the money until the child is age 18.

2. Education IRAs — $2,000/year can be contributed per child; however, the biggest benefit is taxes — there are none. As long as the money in an Education IRA is used for some sort of higher education, then absolutely no taxes are paid on the growth — a very good deal! Although $2,000/year may or may not sound like a lot of money, if a parent or grandparent were to start contributing when the child is born, assuming the money were invested properly*, the Education IRA could potentially grow to just shy of $240,000 after 20 years, probably enough to pay for the entire cost of higher education.

My advice to grandparents is to stop buying savings bonds for your grandchildren and start funding an Education IRA. It makes more sense — and dollars!

$2,000/year invested in an S&P 500 Index Fund 20 years ago. For illustrative purposes only — not guaranteed.

3. Section 529 Plans — State tuition programs, also known as 529 Plans, allow states to set up plans that qualify for certain tax breaks. Beginning in 2002, all withdrawals from State 529 college savings plans will be tax-free, as long as the money is used for higher education. Another key benefit is that mom and dad never lose control of the assets. Because no two state plans are exactly alike, check with your state's Department of Education and request a free booklet on Section 529 Plans. You do not have to set up your 529 Plan in the state you reside. You can choose a plan from any state that best fits your needs and personality.

When you start an UGMA, Education IRA, or a 529 Plan, you must pick the investment vehicle (a place where the money will be invested). It's like funding an IRA. You can open one in a bank, insurance company, brokerage house, or mutual fund. You have the same choices with college funding. It is my opinion that the best investment vehicle for funding college is a mutual fund. Since there are over 10,000 mutual funds to choose from, you should get sound advice from a qualified advisor. Please, no "hot tips."

#10 — Prepare for a Nursing Home

Congress has passed several laws over the years to make it harder to give away or hide assets from being taken by a nursing home. According to statistics I read recently, there is a 48% chance that a 65-year-old will enter a nursing home. If both husband and wife are living, odds are one will enter a home. I don't know about you, but that scares me! The cost per day in my area for nursing home care is almost $300/day. Most people cannot afford such an expense. My suggestion is to purchase Long-Term Care (LTC) Insurance while you're healthy and while you're young. Both my wife and I purchased LTC insurance before we turned 50. If there is nearly a 50% chance of going into a home before we die, I do not want to risk losing everything to a nursing home! Since we are both relatively young, the annual cost for a good LTC policy is under $500/year for each of us. As far as I'm concerned, it's money well spent, even though I hope I never have the opportunity to use it.

I hear a lot of excuses on why not to buy a nursing home policy. For example, "Medicare takes care of the nursing home." Wrong! Medicare coverage is generally limited to 100 days and then only if admission follows a hospital stay. (Custodial care is not covered.) "I'm a veteran. The V.A. will take care of me." Wrong again! The V.A. will not provide custodial care. "My family will take care of me." Maybe – if they are still alive and healthy when you need the care. If you need around-the-clock care, how many family members will it take?

Is Long-Term Care insurance right for you?

You should NOT buy Long-Term Care Insurance if:

- You can't afford the premiums

- You have limited assets

- Your only source of income is a Social Security benefit or Supplemental Security Income (SSI)

- You often have trouble paying for utilities, food, medicine, or other important needs

Financial Planning 101

You should CONSIDER buying Long-Term Care Insurance if:

- You have significant assets and income
- You want to protect some of your assets and income
- You want to pay for your own care
- You want to stay independent of the support of others

Source: © 1999 National Association of Insurance Commissioners

Not preparing for a nursing home expense is like taking your entire net worth, walking up to a roulette wheel in a casino, and putting it all on red. You have a 50/50 chance of losing it all — about the same odds as going into a nursing home. Why take the chance? You've worked hard for what you have. Why give it away to a nursing home when you can buy insurance to protect what you have! It's never too late to start managing your money responsibly and to start planning for the future.

Treat Your Children Well
They Will Eventually Choose Your Nursing Home

Putting a comprehensive financial plan together is not easy, but it's worth it. My advice is to find a qualified financial planner to help you accomplish your financial goals (see Resource Section in Chapter 9). If, on the other hand, you're a do-it-yourselfer, I would suggest reading a couple of books on the subject (see Suggested Reading in Chapter 9) or seeking help from someone you know who is already financially successful. Putting your own financial plan together is like riding a bicycle for the first time – you'll no doubt fall off a couple of times and scrape your knees. As long as you don't give up and keep trying, you'll eventually get the hang of it. If you don't like pain (losing money), then getting professional help can be less painful. Either way — get started sooner than later!

Put a financial team together. A CPA, attorney, investment specialist, and insurance expert make a good solid foundation to your dream team.

"Plans fail for lack of counsel, but with many advisors they succeed." (Proverbs 15:22)

Is lack of proper planning keeping you out of the Promised Land?

Chapter 8

Final Thoughts:
A Call To Action

Whatever happened to the Promised Land? Nothing! It's still waiting for those who will to enter in. God has clearly (through His Word) given us directions on how to get there. Most of us ignore His directions and choose to try to get there our own way. That's the way it was back in the Garden of Eden (our will, not His), and that's the way it still is today. "I want to do it my way." The Promised Land, my metaphor for financial freedom, is available to anyone willing to follow God's directions and to those who are willing to pay the price.

Remember, once the Israelites entered in, they still had many battles to fight. Obtaining financial freedom is not easy, but it is well worth it. The alternative, financial bondage, is far less appealing. Wandering in the desert (struggling financially) for the rest of one's life is not my idea of living. Money is a tool. We, as stewards, are to use this tool God has entrusted us with to build something wonderful and lasting. Tools can be used to build something worthwhile, for demolition or destruction, or they can lie idle and rust until useless. It's the same tool, but it is our choice how we use it. How will you make the best use of what God has given you?

Dreams, Goals, and Vision are Worthless Unless Followed By Action

Take a few minutes and imagine what your life would be like without debt, without car payments, installment loans, equity loans, mortgage payments, or credit card bills. What would it be like to not rush to the bank every Friday to deposit your paycheck to cover the checks you wrote out Wednesday? How would you feel if you were able to pay cash for all of your purchases, to be able to bless your church, missionaries, evangelists, the homeless and the needy? Accumulating wealth is good if it is used to bring joy to others!

Be a person of vision, not just a dreamer.
—Anonymous

What's keeping you out of the Promised Land? Is it lack of knowledge? That may have been a legitimate reason before reading this book; there is no excuse now. Is it lack of faith? I hear people say they don't have faith. I disagree. Everyone has faith. If you get in an elevator, drive over a bridge, or get into an airplane, bus, or train, you have faith. Believe, and God will help you take the first steps.

Is it lack of action? The scripture says in James 1:22, *"But be ye doers of the Word, and not hearers only, deceiving your own selves."* Again, in James 4:17, *"Therefore to him that knoweth to do good and doeth it not, to him it is sin."* Jesus said in Matthew 7:24, *"Therefore whosoever heareth these sayings of mine, and doeth them, I will liken him to a wise man."* Verse 26 continues, *"And everyone that heareth these sayings of mine, and doeth them not shall be likened unto a foolish man."* The Bible says in James 2:20 that *"Faith without works is dead."*

Final Thoughts – A Call to Action

Unfortunately, When All Is Said And Done More Is Said Than Is Done

I recently had the privilege of meeting the legendary basketball coach from UCLA, John Wooden, a great motivator who led his teams to ten NCAA national championships – something no one has ever done, and, in all likelihood, will never be repeated! He is a man of both wisdom and faith. When he was asked in his first year of coaching what his secret was for turning his team from worst to first in the PAC 8 (now the PAC 10), he replied, "There is no progress without change."

If you want to progress into the Promised Land –then change!

Do you really want to wander in the desert, live in a tent, and eat manna for the next 40 years? Think about it. Unless you take action, unless you change, you'll be in the same financial state four decades from now. If those prospects are depressing and you get a sick feeling in the pit of your stomach, then do something about it. Financial success is a choice. It doesn't just happen. Take the road less traveled. Not asking for directions is a "man thing." (It must have been handed down from Moses.) This book is your road map. It's up to you to follow the directions. I have found that making excuses is easier than becoming financially independent, but that's not what God intended for you.

THE TRUTH IS, GOD WANTS YOU TO LIVE IN HIS PROMISED LAND! Will you enter in? Persist until you succeed!

Opportunity Takes Up With Those Who Recognize It

"And let us not get tired of doing what is right, for after a while we will reap a harvest of blessing if we don't get discouraged and give up." (Galatians 6:9)

"Therefore, my beloved brethren, be ye steadfast, unmovable, always abounding in the work of the Lord, forasmuch as ye know that your labor is not in vain in the Lord." (I Cor. 15:58)

Whatever Happened to the Promised Land?

"Wait on the Lord, and keep His way and He shall exalt thee to inherit the land." (Psalm 37:34)

Here are some additional "tidbits" to motivate you to start your journey to the Promised Land:

1. If you settle for what you've got, you deserve what you get.

2. The definition of insanity is doing the same things over and over, and expecting a different result. (Interpretation: If you won't change, neither will your current economic condition.)

3. If it is to be, it is up to me. (God will help, but you must take the initiative.)

4. If you continue to do what you have always done, you will continue to get what you have always got.

5. You never know how much time you have left. That's why you need to do all you can do while you can still do it.

Here is all the encouragement you should need:

I came from a poor family and grew up in the projects, with no financial background or expertise. I was in debt "up to my eyebrows" less than 25 years ago. So, if I could do it, SO CAN YOU!! It's as easy as A-B-C:

"A" – Allow the Holy Spirit to speak to you, teach, guide, and direct you.

"B" – Believe God wants you to live in the Promised Land, to prosper and bless you and your family.

"C" – Change! Unless you do, your financial circumstances won't.

Final Exhortation

There is no one more knowledgeable on the subject of money than God. There is no one wiser on the subject of money than God. There is no one more trustworthy when it comes to money than God. There is no one else I would rather obey when it comes to money than God.

If you're truly sick and tired of being sick and tired when it comes to your lack of money, then educate yourself, trust God, obey His Word, work hard, don't give up, and you will enter into the Promised Land! Remember – you are never a failure until you quit!

See you there!

"If you abide in Me, and My words abide in you, you will ask what you desire, and it shall be done for you. By this My Father is glorified, that you bear much fruit; so you will be My disciples." (John 15:7&8)

"Let us hear the conclusion of the whole matter: Fear God, and keep his commandments, for this is the whole duty of man." (Ecclesiastes 12:13)

"For it was I, Jehovah your God, who brought you out of the land of Egypt. Open your mouth wide and see if I won't fill it. You will receive every blessing you can use! But no, my people won't listen. Israel doesn't want me around. So I am letting them go their blind and stubborn way, living according to their own desires. But oh, that my people would listen to me!" (Psalms 81:10-13)

We Will Either Find A Way Or Make One
—Hannibal

Chapter 9

It's Not WHAT You Know
It's WHO You Know!

It's important to understand for whom the Promised Land was intended. The entire pretext of *Whatever Happened to the Promised Land?* is that, in order to enter in, you must be a Christian. The "Promised Land" was originally intended for the Israelites and then those of us who were "grafted in" (Romans 11:17) to the kingdom of God. How does one become a Christian and then, therefore, have the right to the Promised Land? By being "saved" or born again. Follow these simple instructions from the Bible, and you can start your journey:

In order to go to heaven, you must experience a rebirth. In John 3:7, Jesus said to Nicodemus, *"Ye must be born again."* In the Bible, God gives us the plan of how to be born again, which means to be saved. His plan is simple! You can be saved today. How? First, you must realize you are a sinner. "For all have sinned, and come short of the glory of God" (Romans 3:23). Because we are all sinners, we are condemned to death. "For the wages (payment) of sin is death" (Romans 6:23). This includes eternal separation from God in Hell. *"…it is appointed unto men once to die, but after this the judgment."* (Hebrews 9:27)."

But God loved you so much He gave His only begotten Son, Jesus, to bear your sin and die in your place. "…He hath made Him [Jesus, Who knew no sin] to be sin for us … that we might be made the righteousness of God in Him (2 Cor. 5:21)." Jesus had to shed His blood and die. "For the life of the flesh is in the blood (Lev. 17:11)." "…without shedding of blood is no remission [pardon] (Hebrews 9:22)." "…But God commendeth His love toward us, in that, while we were yet sinners, Christ died for us" (Romans 5:8).

Although we cannot understand how, God said my sins and your sins were laid upon Jesus and He died in our place. He became our substitute. It is true. God cannot lie. My friend, "God… now commandeth all men everywhere to repent (Acts 17:30)." This repentance is a change of mind that agrees with God that one is a sinner and also agrees with what Jesus did for us on the Cross. Simply believe on Him as the one who bore your sin, died in your place, was buried, and whom God resurrected.

In Acts 16:30-31, the Philippian jailer asked Paul and Silas: "… 'Sirs, what must I do to be saved?' And they said, 'Believe on the Lord Jesus Christ, and thou shalt be saved…'" His resurrection powerfully assures that the believer can claim everlasting life when Jesus is received as Savior. "But as many as received Him, to them gave He power to become the sons of God, even to them that believe on His name (John 1:12)." "For whosoever shall call upon the name of the Lord shall be saved (Romans 10:13)."

"Whosoever" includes you. "Shall be saved" means not maybe, nor can, but *shall* be saved.

Right now, wherever you are, repent. Lift your heart to God in prayer. In Luke 18:13, the sinner prayed: "God be merciful to me a sinner."

Just pray:

"Oh, God, I know I am a sinner. I believe Jesus was my substitute when He died on the Cross. I believe His shed blood, death, burial, and resurrection were for me. I now receive Him as my Savior. I thank You for the forgiveness of my sins, the gift of salvation and everlasting life, because of Your merciful grace. Amen."

Just take God at His word and claim His salvation by faith. Believe, and you will be saved. No church, no lodge, no good works can save you. Remember, God does the saving. All of it! God's simple plan of salvation is: You are a sinner. Therefore, unless you believe on Jesus who died in your place, you will spend eternity in hell. If you believe on Him as your crucified, buried, and risen Savior, you receive forgiveness for all of your sins and His gift of eternal salvation by faith. You say, "Surely, it cannot be that simple." Yes, it's that simple! It is scriptural. It is God's plan. My friend, believe on Jesus and receive Him as Savior today. If His plan is not perfectly clear, read this section over and over, without laying it down until you understand it. Your soul is worth more than all the world.

"For what shall it profit a man, if he shall gain the whole world, and lose his own soul (Mark 8:36)?" Be sure you are saved. If you lose your soul, you miss Heaven and lose all. Please! Let God save you this very moment. God's power will save you, help keep you saved, and enable you to live a victorious Christian life. "There hath no temptation taken you but such as is common to man: but God is faithful, Who will not suffer you to be tempted above that ye are able; but will with the temptation also make a way to escape, that ye may be able to bear it (I Corinthians 10:13)."

Do not trust your feelings; they change. Stand on God's promises. They never change. After you are saved, there are three things to practice daily for spiritual growth:

1. Pray – you talk to God.
2. Read your Bible – God talks to you.
3. Witness – you talk for God.

You should be baptized in obedience to the Lord Jesus Christ as a public testimony of your salvation, and then unite with a Bible-believing church without delay. "Be not thou therefore ashamed of the testimony of our Lord… (2 Timothy 1:8). "Whosoever therefore shall confess (testify of) Me before men, him will I confess also before My Father which is in heaven (Matthew 10:32)."

Ford Porter – God's Simple Plan of Salvation © 1991 - paraphrased

Chapter 10

Recommended Reading List & Other Helpful Resources For Improving Your Financial I.Q.

As I'm laying on the beach here in sunny Cancun, Mexico, attempting to put the final touches on this "brainchild" of mine, called *Whatever Happened to the Promised Land?*, it occurred to me that I should help you to take the next step. I assume you want to do so.

Before I share with you a list of various reading materials that have helped me to obtain financial independence, let me share with you an epiphany I had here on the beach. I spend a lot of time on the beach. It's relaxing, warm, and quieter than my office. I get to read, re-energize, and take it easy. I also get the opportunity to take a step back and reflect on the important areas of life, such as family, church, career, and my relationship with the Lord. I assure you, the best place to handle this "heady stuff" is on the beach. But here's the "rub" — why is everyone else here on the beach reading those fictional romance novels, scary Stephen King books, or John Grisham suspense stories? I'm sure they are entertaining, but they have little to do with reality. What are you feeding your brain?

The same is true about television. You know the saying, "Garbage in, garbage out." Why not feed your brain any number of good books on money, finance, or investing? We all deal with money every day of our lives. Why not learn how to use it, spend it, and save it wisely? Why not learn how to have money work for you instead of you working for it? I'm not talking about a finance degree — just learn the basics and master using them. Fiction, by its very definition, is not real. Why do we want to spend our time on things that are not real and have no relevance to our day-to-day living? What's wrong with reality? How about getting real when it comes to obtaining financial savvy, educating yourself, and your family? Becoming financially free is not all that difficult, but it doesn't happen all by itself either.

There are countless books and resources available on money, investing, budgeting, and stewardship — here are but a few. Why not start your journey today?

An Investment In Knowledge Always
Pays The Best Interest
—Benjamin Franklin

Helpful Resources
For Improving Your Financial I.Q.

Learn to Earn, Peter Lynch

One Up On Wall Street, Peter Lynch

Beating the Street, Peter Lynch

Rich Dad Poor Dad, Robert Kiyosaki

Preparing for Retirement, Larry Burkett

Recommended Reading and Helpful Resources

The Roaring 2000s, Harry S. Dent

Stocks for the Long Run, Jeremy Siegel

The Templeton Plan, John Templeton

The New Money Masters, John Train

Titan, Ron Chernow

Business Buy the Bible, Wade Cook

Buffet, the Making of an American Capitalist, Roger Lowenstein

The Retiree's Complete Guide to the Secrets of a Secure & Peaceful Retirement, R. Richard Everett**

Chance Favors The Informed Mind
—Louis Pasteur

*The suggested reading material listed previously is for educational purposes. Always seek professional advice before investing or attempting complex financial planning.

Resources — Feed Your Brain

Crown Financial Ministries
Larry Burkett - www.crown.org

Consumer Credit Counseling Service
800-388-2227

Financial Planning Association
They will provide a list of Certified Financial Planners in your area.
Telephone: 800-322-4237 Web Site: www.fpanet.org

Internal Revenue Service
You can order free publications explaining the tax laws by calling 800-829-3676. Tax law information and publications are also available on the IRS Web site www.irs.gov. Frequently ordered publications include:

Pub. No.	Title
523	Tax Information on Selling Your Home
550	Investment Income and Expenses
551	Basis of Assets
554	Tax Information for Older Americans
564	Mutual Fund Distributions
575	Pension and Annuity Income
590	IRAs
915	Social Security Benefits
950	Estate & Gift Taxes

International Association for Registered Financial Consultants (IARFC).

They will provide a list of qualified registered financial consultants. 800-532-9060; www.IARFCwebsites.com

Morningstar®
Providers of news and analyses on markets, stocks, and mutual funds. 800-735-0700; www.morningstar.com

Social Security Administration
For information on Social Security, call the Social Security Administration (SSA) and ask for the Request for Earnings and Benefit Estimate Statement. By sending the completed form to the SSA, you will receive a statement showing your Social Security earnings history, the amount paid in Social Security taxes, and an estimate of the Social Security benefits due to you when eligible. The SSA offers numerous free, short publications that describe their programs. Call your local Social Security office or 800-772-1213, or visit the Social Security web site at www.ssa.gov.

The Society of Certified Senior Advisors (SCSA)
They will provide a list of certified senior consultants in your area. The society educates professionals on the health, economic, and social issues that seniors face. 800-653-1785; www.society-CSA.com

Value Line Mutual Fund Survey
Obtain full-page reports on 1,500 mutual funds that include 20 years of performance data, standard deviation, Value Line ranking, and portfolio manager ranking. 800-634-3583; www.valueline.com

Investment Publications

Barron's: 800-544-0422; www.barrons.com

Business Week: 800-635-1200; www.businessweek.com

Investor's Business Daily: 800-831-2525; www.investors.com

Wall Street Journal: 800-544-0422; wsj.com

Fortune: 800-621-8000; www.fortune.com

With All Thy Getting, Get Understanding
—B. C. Forbes

Chapter 11

About the Author

R. Richard Everett is the founder and president of the Everett Financial Group, Inc. Mr. Everett has been in the financial services industry since 1984 and served as a Senior Vice President for one of the nation's largest financial services company for three years prior to starting the Everett Financial Group, Inc. The Everett Financial Group, Inc. has since grown to be one of the area's largest and most respected financial planning firms.

Mr. Everett is a Registered Financial Consultant (RFC), a Certified Senior Advisor (CSA), and is a member of the Financial Planning Association (FPA). He was named Financial Planner of the Year for 1996 by First Financial Planners, Inc.

In addition to conducting hundreds of investment seminars throughout Connecticut, he has taught financial planning courses to municipal employees in several communities. Mr. Everett has appeared numerous times on WTNH, the local affiliate for ABC television, and he has hosted his own 30-minute financial planning television show on NHTV, the North Haven cable station. He has hosted his own one-hour weekly radio show on WELI and has co-authored two financial books, as well as having numerous financial articles published.

Mr. Everett is licensed with the National Association of Security Dealers in several states and holds an insurance license with the State of Connecticut.

Richard & MarySue Everett have been married since 1976. They have two children, Jennifer & Shawn. The Everetts attend church at Church on the Rock in New Haven, CT and are residents of North Haven, CT. Richard has also donated time to work with local churches and Sage Services, a United Way program, to help people in need of basic budgeting and financial counseling. He has also served on several non-profit organizational boards, including Teen Challenge and the Luis Palau Evangelistic Association.

Richard Everett travels the country speaking to congregations on financial management and stewardship. For questions or comments regarding stewardship, or to schedule a speaking engagement with Mr. Everett, please send an e-mail to: rreverett1952@yahoo.com or call 203-506-9708. You can also visit us at:

www.sowfarsowgoodministries.com

Index of
Basic Financial Terms

Asset Allocation: Asset allocation means spreading your investments over different types of investment categories. By taking advantage of this concept, you can invest some assets for safety, some for income, and some for growth.

Asset Class: A group of investments considered similar in potential risk and return. There are three basic asset classes: stocks, bonds, and short-term securities (or cash).

Assets: Assets are the property and resources (such as cash and investments) of a person or company. A mutual fund's assets include whatever securities (stocks, bonds, Treasury bills, etc.) it owns, plus any cash.

Whatever Happened to the Promised Land?

Bear Market: A term signifying a decline in the market.

Bid and Asked: The bid is the price offered at any time for a security or commodity, and the ask is the price requested. The quote, also known as the quotation, is the bid and asking on a security or commodity. For instance, a quote on a given stock may be 20.25 bid and 20.50 asked. In other words, the highest price a buy wanted to pay was $20.25, and the lowest the seller was willing to take was $20.50.

Blue Chip: A stock that is low-risk because the company has a reputation for reliability, quality and the ability to make money and pay dividends.

Bonds: Bonds are essentially loans – or debt. They're issued by corporations, governments, or municipalities to raise money. A bond certificate is like an IOU; it shows the amount loaned (principal), the rate of interest to be paid on the loan, and the date that the principal will be paid back (maturity date). Mutual funds that invest primarily in bonds are called "income" funds.

Broker: An agent who has passed a test to determine his basic knowledge in securities, who is registered with the S.E.C., and who may charge a fee to buy and sell securities, commodities, and other properties for the public.

Bull Market: The term used to express a rise in the market.

Common Stocks: When people talk about a company's stock, they usually mean common stock. When you own common stock in a company, you share in its success or failure. As part owner, you vote on important policy issues, such as picking the board of directors. If the company prospers, you may get part of the profits, called dividends. Also, the value of your shares of the company may go up; common stock generally has the greatest potential for growth. However, it also carries the greatest risk, since that value can drop if the company does poorly. If the company goes bankrupt, common stockholders are the last to receive any payment.

Index of Basic Financial Terms

Compounding: When you put money in the bank, it earns interest. When that interest earns interest, the result is "compound" interest. Of course, investing in a retirement plan is different from putting money in the bank, but you still get the benefits of compounding. For example, if income from bonds (or dividends from stocks or mutual funds) is reinvested into your account, the earnings compound as well. Compounding can help your balance increase.

Convertible Bond: Bonds which at the option of the holder may be converted into other securities of the corporation. When bonds are convertible into stocks, the stocks into which they are convertible must be authorized at the time the bonds are issued.

The owner of the convertible bond will find it profitable to exercise his or her option if the value of the stock into which it is being converted should subsequently exceed the value of the bond at the conversion price. The price of the bond usually relates to the price of the securities into which it is convertible.

Convertible bonds are attractive because they allow the purchaser the safety of a bond or an increase in value through the conversion option. The corporation gains whenever a conversion to securities takes place because the fixed charges of the corporate debt are reduced.

Diversification: This concept of spreading your money across different kinds of investments could potentially moderate your investment risk. It's the idea of not putting all your eggs in one basket. A diversified portfolio can help shield you from large losses because even if some securities falter, others may perform well. However, diversification cannot protect against loss.

Dividend: The amount of payment decided by the board of directors to be made to the shareholder for each share held. Preferred shareholders generally receive a fixed amount, which was determined when the preferred share was issued.

Dollar Cost Averaging: This is a method of investing. Money is invested at regular intervals in the same investment. Because you invest the same amount each time, you automatically buy less of the investment when its price is lower. Though the method doesn't guarantee a profit or guard against loss in declining markets, the average cost of each share is usually lower than if you buy at random times. For dollar cost averaging to work, you must continue to invest regularly over time and purchase shares in both market ups and downs.

Dow Jones Industrial Average: A stock market average reached by a rather complicated formula. The average is calculated on the basis of 30 major industrial corporations whose total closing prices are divided by a number, which compensates for past stock splits and stock dividends.

Equity: This means ownership in a company. When you own shares of stock of a company, it also means that you own equity in that company. So stock investments are also called "equities." Similarly, mutual funds that invest in stocks are often called "equity funds."

401(k): Under section 401(k) of the Internal Revenue Code, employees can set aside money for retirement on a pretax basis through a plan sponsored by their employer. To encourage saving for retirement through these plans, the federal government created special tax advantages for 401(k) contributions.

Ginnie Mae: A nickname for Government National Mortgage Association. Similar to modified pass-thru mortgage securities; these are guaranteed by the government.

Index/Benchmark: An index measures the price and performance of a specific group of stocks. There are many indexes that in investor can track each business day, including:

The Dow Jones Industrial Average: A formula that represents the stock prices of 30 major industrial companies in the United. States. Because it includes companies that represent core sectors of our economy, the Dow is considered the most accepted indicator of overall market performance. When the Dow is up, it means the prices of these companies rose during the day; when it's down, these prices fell.

Index of Basic Financial Terms

The S&P 500® Index – an index of 500 widely held U.S. stocks. The Standard & Poor's Corporation calculates the market prices of these stocks, including the reinvestment of dividends, as a way to track the overall performance of the stock market.

Inflation: When the price of goods and services rises over time, the result is called inflation. This means that things you buy today will cost more in the future.

Investment Mix: The combination of investment options you choose.

Investment Option Types: Each option has its owns investment objective, based on a targeted level of investment risk and return. There are several types of investment options:

Asset allocation funds spread their assets among the three general investment categories, including short-term instruments, bonds, and equities (stocks). They gradually adjust this mix of investments as market conditions change.

Balanced funds buy a mix of common stocks, preferred stocks, and bonds. Their goal is to blend long-term growth from stocks with income from dividends.

Growth funds invest mostly in the stocks of different types of companies, both foreign and domestic.

Growth and income funds invest in different types of bonds and stocks of both foreign and domestic companies.

Income funds, or "bond funds," purchase bonds of different types, maturities, and quality.

International funds usually invest the majority of their assets in stocks or bonds of companies and governments outside the United States.

Managed income funds are not mutual funds. They aim to preserve an investor's principal while earning interest income through investment contracts and other fixed-income arrangements with major financial institutions. These investment options are not guaranteed by the plan sponsor or the fund manager and are not FDIC insured.

Money market funds purchase high-quality, short-term money market instruments such as certificates of deposit (CDs). An investment in a money market fund is not insured or guaranteed by the FDIC or any other government agency. Although the money market funds seek to preserve the value of your investment at $1 per share, it is possible to lose money by investing in these funds.

Investment Risk: The chance that you may lose a portion of your investment principal.

Issuer: A company, government, or municipality that offers bonds to investors. (See Bonds.)

Junk Bond: Bond in default, or bond considered high-risk because of low rating.

Management Styles: There are three levels of management that can apply to a plan's investment options:

Active management means that a portfolio manager is trying to outperform the market. Whatever the market does, as measured by certain benchmarks, the manager will try to do better and increase value for investors.

Passive management means that a portfolio manager is trying to achieve a return for investor that is comparable to the return of the overall market or an index.

Unmanaged is when it is not necessary for a professional manager to make "buy/sell" decisions because investment decisions are driven by participant-directed cash flows and plan sponsor direction, like unitized company stock funds are.

Margin Account: A type of account where a customer borrows money to pay for a certain percentage of the cost of securities. The margin is the money borrowed. The broker may use his or her credit to borrow the money from the bank for the customer's account; there is a charge for borrowing this money. The broker holds the securities for the customer as collateral. The Federal Reserve sets the maximum amount, which may be borrowed. Margin requirements may be lowered to induce more trading or raised if the government fears overbuying or speculation fever.

Margin accounts are also used in commodity future trading. They are risky because if the stock goes down, the customer is required to add money to maintain the margin.

NASD: Abbreviation of National Association of Security Dealers, Inc. An organization for brokers and dealers in the over-the-counter securities business.

NASDAQ: Abbreviation of National Association of Securities Dealers Automated Quotations. An electronic system that provides brokers and dealers belonging to NASD with price quotations on securities traded over-the- counter.

No-load Fund: An investment company that does not make a sales charge for the purchase of its shares.

Odd Lot: Stocks traded in units of under 100.

Off Board: A term used for securities not executed on a national securities exchange but rather over-the-counter.

Open-end Fund: An investment company that continually issues shares as it receives new capital or that stands ready to redeem shares at net asset value.

Option: The right to buy or sell at a specific price within a given time.

Over-the-counter: Method of issuing securities for those companies which may not meet the requirements for trading on the Big Board or their regional exchanges. The dealers may or may not be members of a securities exchange, but must be members of the National Association of Security Dealers.

Penny stocks: Stocks selling at less than 3 dollars a share. These are mostly over-the-counter stocks and may be speculative.

Pension Plans: Also known as defined benefit retirement plans, these provide a specified amount of money after you retire following a set number of years of service (in other words, the benefit is "defined" in advance). Once you retire, the amount you receive is fixed and usually does not increase with inflation.

Portfolio: A portfolio is a collection of securities and other investments. Your "investment portfolio" refers to your investments within the plan.

Preferred stock: Stock promising prior claim on the company's earnings. Dividends are paid at a specified time before common stock shareholders receive theirs, and in case of liquidation, preferred stockholders have priority in all claims. Preferred stock may be participating, cumulative, or convertible.

Price-earnings ratio: The formula whereby the cost of a stock is divided by its earnings for a 12-month period. XYZ common stock sells on the market for $30 and pays $2 dividend. The price-earnings ratio is 15 to 1.

Prospectus: A prospectus provides investors with a thorough description of a mutual fund. It explains the fund's objective, how it invests its money, and describes fees and expenses associated with the fund. You should read a fund's prospectus before choosing your investment.

Return: This is the rate an investment earns – it's expressed as a percentage. It generally refers to the change in value (increase or decrease in share or unit price) and any income earned on the investment over a period of time. It's a way of comparing investments.

Securities: This term refers to all investment options, including stocks, bonds, and short-term securities, and shares of mutual funds, etc.

Index of Basic Financial Terms

SIPC: Abbreviation of Securities Investor Protection Corporation which provides funds, when necessary, to protect member firms' customers' equity.

Split: Agreement voted by the directors of the corporation and approved by its shareholders to divide the outstanding shares into a greater number of shares, such as 2 for 1; the equity remains the same. Ann Smith owns 100 shares of XZ stock selling for $50 a share. After the 2 for 1 split, Ann Smith owns 200 shares of XZ stock at $25 a share.

Standard and Poor's Stock Price Index (S&P Index): Index similar to Dow Jones Industrial Average, except Standard and Poor uses not 30 industrial corporations, but 500 major corporations consisting of 425 industrials, 25 railroads, and 55 utilities, all listed on the New York Stock Exchange.

Stock: A company sells stock to raise money. When individuals or when companies buy stocks, they become owners of a part of the corporation issuing the stock. This ownership is called "equity."

Tax-deferred Contributions: The amount you choose to have deducted from your paycheck and contributed into your retirement savings plan. Your contributions are deducted from your paycheck before income taxes are taken out, which reduces your current taxable income. Taxes will be due on these contributions when you withdraw them from the plan.

Tender offer: Request by a corporation—under specific terms and for a certain time period—for the public, and other stockholders such as institutions, to surrender their stocks—usually at a price higher than the current market.

Treasury bill or note also known as T-bill: A non-interest-bearing discount security issued by the U.S> Treasury to finance the National Debt. The income in discount bills is in the increase between the purchase price, which is discounted, and the full maturity value. If, for instance, the Treasury decides to offer issues of $1,000 notes discounted at 10 percent, the purchaser would only pay $900 (10 percent of $1,000 equals $100;

$1,000 less $100 equals $900) and receive $1,000 at maturity. Treasury bills are fully taxable. The minimum round lot is $10,000.

U.S. Savings Bonds: The term that usually refers to a series of bonds issued by the federal government. Some series are discount type; The income from these bonds is taxable. Sometimes the government refers to these series by letters such as "E" and "H."

Yield: The yield is the effective interest rate or dividend on an investment.

Sources:

Fidelity Investments Institutional Service Corp., Inc.
Monarch's Dictionary of Investment Terms

Footnotes

1. Chapter 4

   *Footnote: 1980 figures from the Automotive News Market Data Book.

   2006 figures are from Car and Driver.

2. Chapter 6

   *Footnote: Investments must be regular and the same amount each time. If the investor discontinues the plan when the market value is less than the cost of the shares, he or she will lose money. The investor must be willing and able to invest during the low price levels. This plan does not protect the investor in a steadily declining market.

3. Chapter 7

   [1]Source: Tax Foundation

   [2]Charitable deduction limits: Gifts of cash are deductible up to 50% of a taxpayer's AGI. Gifts of securities and real estate are deductible up to 30% AGI. Any excess deductions can be carried forward and deducted over an additional five years.

   [3]May be subject to a vesting schedule.

GATEKEEPER PUBLISHING

is expanding its authorship with the launch of our new imprint

'Think Big, Little Books.'

We are looking for fresh, cutting-edge manuscripts that have a relevant message for this hour.

To submit your manuscrip, visit:
www.gatekeeperpublishing.com

You can download a manuscript submission form on our Publishing page.

Are you a published author trying to make a living writing books?

Consider joining the GateKeeper family of authors. Be a part of a company setting new industry standards. We commit aggressive marketing budgets to every project and give our authors the highest royalties in the trade.

Whatever your situation, GateKeeper can offer you numerous options to suite your specific needs. We offer a full range of services including:

- Complete "book publishing" – from concept to completion

- Innovative Graphics, and full cover design services

- Audio Book Productions

- Foreign Language book production, transcriptions and more

To see our full range of services, or for information on submitting your manuscript, visit our web site. You can find our downloadable Manuscript Submission Form on the "Publishing" page.

www.gatekeeperpublishing.com